Synagogues
of the First Century C.E.

Deslee Campbell

For Professor Boaz Zissu, with thanks.

Chapter 1: Synagogues in Judea

Chapter 2: Synagogues in Galilee

Chapter 3: Overall Conclusions

Preamble

According to the New Testament, by the early 1st century of the Common Era (the period of Jesus and his Apostles) the synagogue had become an established and semi-formalised institution in Galilee. As recently as the 1960s, however, it was believed that this did not apply in Judea or anywhere within easy access to the Temple because they would be superfluous. Furthermore there was *"no data to indicate that the synagogue was an important institute alongside the Temple"*.[1] Some scholars even doubted the existence of separate buildings for Jewish teaching or worship. [2]

Since Israel's victory in the Six Day War of 1967, Israeli national sentiment has expressed itself in an interest in the ancient past of the Jewish people so that amateur archaeology became more an obsession than a hobby and access to previously closed areas has become available: especially David's city (Orphel) and the Jewish quarter of the Old City. These days, in Israel's busy archaeological digging season, foreign and local teams are constantly at work throughout the country and important discoveries are often found. For Christians, also, knowledge of if and how these discoveries shed light upon Bible-narrative is important. The discovery of numerous 1st-century synagogue buildings since the 1960's is therefore of interest to both Jews and Christians: they are part of our shared heritage.

The oldest synagogue in Israel, in Jericho, was destroyed by an earthquake before the turn of the eras so is not discussed here.[3]

Any map of where the early synagogues were built will show they form two distinct clusters. Contrary to what might be expected by readers of the Gospels, the oldest synagogues discovered so far are not in Galilee, but in Judea where there are five from the 1st century C.E. (A.D.); possibly more. There is another cluster in Galilee, with perhaps seven examples. The total is slowly increasing although not all are equally well preserved or easy to date.

In most cases the dating is undeniable as most of them were destroyed by the Roman army in c.70 C.E. and never rebuilt, although some were repaired and continued to be used until the second decimation by the Roman army, called the Bar Kokhba War, of 132-135 C.E.

Numerous pre-destruction synagogue-remnants have recently been found in Israel. They provide an ever-growing body of evidence to excite academic study and they support the New Testament's claim that synagogues were widespread.

Those in Judea will be considered first. The oldest evidence in Judea and the first relevant discovery was found in Jerusalem: an inscription and some items of decoration but no monumental remains. This is known as the 'Theodotus' inscription which tells us a little about his rebuilt synagogue, the early version of which was run by his grandfather and then his father: three generations of priests who were also rulers of this synagogue.

In other examples, the floor-plan of early synagogues is known because the flooring has generally survived, perhaps also with a few courses of the stone walls. Some were created very late in the piece: just before the destruction of 70 C.E. By contrast a number date to before the turn of the eras (from B.C.E. to C.E. i.e., B.C. to A.D.).

Each significant excavation demonstrates that many well-known scholars were forced into error through lack of hard evidence because scholars can only interpret what they have at hand. One error was that the New Testament was incorrect in stating that there were synagogues throughout Galilee. Another was that synagogues were not purpose-built dedicated buildings but houses etc. used for the purpose, much like a early house-churches. Yet a another error was that 'broadhouse' style synagogues developed later than 'Galilee style' synagogues, whereas the oldest extant architecture yet discovered is 'broadhouse' (Modi'in).

Chapter 1

Synagogues in Judea

1.1: Theodotus Inscription (Jerusalem)

The New Testament is the most useful source of incidental information about the 1st-century synagogues of both modern-day Israel and the Jewish Diaspora of the Eastern Mediterranean. Although the Acts of the Apostles (Acts 6) suggest that there were numerous synagogues in 1st-century Jerusalem to date the only non-literary evidence we have for them is one inscription and some fragments of carved stone that were found in the late 19th century. They had been thrown into a cistern to the South of Temple Mount in Orphel (near David's City).[4] The inscribed stone was found in two large pieces and is very informative but still leaves many questions unanswered.

This stone artefact indicates that Theodotus was the third generation of hereditary leaders of his synagogue,[5] the extensive buildings of which were destroyed, probably by the Romans in 70 C.E.[6] The Greek inscription in question is a basic item in scholars' consideration of 'the synagogue' and suggests some support for the claims in the *Jerusalem Talmud* [7] that there were hundreds of synagogues in the city when Jerusalem was destroyed.[8] There must have been a strong tradition of these, and one that endured for the intervening five hundred years between the Temple and the *Talmud*.

The Theodotus inscription indicates that hospitality for travellers or pilgrims, and provisions for ritual purification, were functions of the Theodotus synagogue but its main purposes were Bible reading and instruction in Torah observance.[9]

It is translated: "Theodotus, son of Vettenus, priest and ruler of the synagogue *(archisynagogus)* son of a ruler of a synagogue *(archisynagogus)* and grandson of a ruler of a synagogue *(archisynagogus)* built the synagogue for the reading of the Law and the teaching of the commandments, and also the guest chamber and the upper rooms and the ritual pools for accommodating those needing them from abroad, which his fathers, the elders and Simonides founded".[10]

Synagogues provided venues for the preaching of Jesus, Paul and other Jesus-believers. The many synagogues in Israel and the Diaspora were a vital part of the preparation for Jesus' coming and the broadcasting of his teaching, and of Paul's preaching, especially in the Jewish Diaspora.

**Plate 1.A. Greek 'Theodotus', Israel Museum, Jerusalem.
Photo: Ian Finnin, 2018.**

As this inscription states that Theodotus was the third generation of hereditary leaders of this Jerusalem synagogue this dates the first building to the 1st-century B.C.E., if not earlier. It functioned until the destruction of 70 C.E. (through 'the Jesus Period' and was a large building, near the Temple, so it would have been seen by Jesus and/or his disciples. This extensive complex had upper and lower chambers (rooms) and pools for ritual immersion.

Theodotus was a priest although priestly-leadership of synagogues was not necessarily the norm. The fact that his synagogue was built, and rebuilt, so near the Temple and existed for three generations, supports the opinion that there was no animosity or competition between the two institutions.

1.2. Modern Modi'in: Was this ancient Modein?

At present the earliest extant synagogue in Israel is at Modi'in, eighteen miles [c.30km] northwest of Jerusalem.

This may well be ancient Modein, the home-town of the priest Mattathias of the House of Hasmon and his five sons, John, Simon, Judah, Eleazar and Jonathan. These five were the Maccabees, who established the Hasmonaean dynasty.[11] Although the family was not Zadokite, three of these Hasmonaean sons became both rulers and high priests in the first generation, and high-priest-king was a role that passed to their descendants down to Antigonus, the last Hasmonaean ruler. He was executed in 37 B.C.E., which gave rise to the reign of Herod the Great.[12]

If this site is not Ancient Modein it is extraordinary to find such an early synagogue built and rebuilt on the same plot of ground in a small, insignificant village. One might expect a synagogue to be in Modein but this building is more remarkable if it is in an obscure, unknown place.

The first phase of the Modi'in rectangular 'hall' is dated c.164 B.C.E (a date shortly after Mattathias settled in the area in c.170 B.C.E.). It was 7m x 3.8m (23' x 12'5") but is difficult to decipher because of later reuse.[13] It was set in a courtyard but it lacked the usual stepped seating and a *mikvah* (ritual bath) and was probably not a synagogue as it was partitioned into three spaces by walls.[14]

The second phase reused some of the previous stonework resulting in a building of 22' x 34' 5" and 37' 9" (or 6.7m x 10.5 and 11.5m).[15] It is dated by coin-finds and pottery to the reigns of the Hasmonaean kings John Hyrcanus (134-104 B.C.E.) or his successor, Alexander Jannaeus (103-76 B.C.E.). This late Hasmonaean rectangular building was a little larger than its predecessor and it did have stepped 'seating' on three sides; but no columns. The floor was paved and there is evidence of secco-technique wall-fresco in red, yellow and white.[16] A small room

(2.5m x 2m or c.8ft x c.6ft) with a beaten-earth floor was added, the courtyard remained and the entrance was moved to the eastern wall.

The top layer of construction, phase three, known by its Arabic name, Umm el-'Umdan, or Mother of the Columns, was dated to the Herodian period (that is, late-1st-century BCE) to as late as the Bar Kokhba period.[17]

Either the second or the third stage functioned throughout 'the Jesus period.' It was damaged by the Romans in c.70 C.E. but was repaired and continued to function until the Bar Kokhba Revolt of c.132 C.E.[18]

In phase 3, three of the existing walls of phase 2 were utilised and it was about 8.6m x 10.5-11.5m.[19] This upper layer was surveyed and recorded by the explorer-diplomat Clermont-Ganneau, in 1873/74. He noted the remains of eight columns, probably sufficient to support an upper storey. A decade later the columns were missing.[20]

This synagogue has stone benches on all four sides, in two, or perhaps three tiers. The floor began, as in previous stages, with tamped earth but this was later plastered over, including over the stepped seating.[21] The dry-walls were of fairly coarse partly-hewn stones with pebbles used to keep the levels even. Walls were painted internally in yellow, red, green and white.

Access was via the previously built courtyard, which had an attached stone bench. Although a second door was cut in the north wall, the main entrance doorway still faced East, towards Jerusalem. This resulted in a building of the 'broad-house style' because its entrance is in the longest wall, opposite which is a raised bema or podium, a square metre in size.

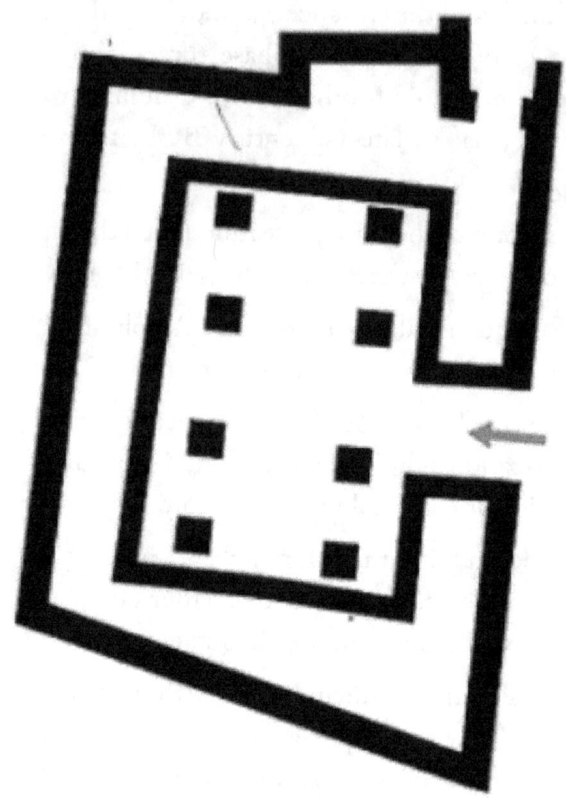

**Plate 1.B. Plan of Modi'in Synagogue.
Design Dept., Shofarot Publications.**

The 'broad-house style' was defined by archaeologist, Michael Avi Yonah, as a late development, which superseded the 'Galilee Style' (which had its entrance on the short wall) but this neat scheme has since proven to be too simplistic.

At this early date in synagogue development, designers were not particular about orientation, the direction faced by the congregation, nor of the front door.

Although these matters have attracted a great deal of 10 debate in scholarship there was no universal or standard plan this early.[22] That was only to come after the widespread destruction of 70 C.E. and the loss of the Temple.[23] At Modi'in a building with storerooms and an enclosed ritual immersion pool (*mikvah*) was added in the courtyard in stage three. Five stairs descend into the bottom of the *mikvah*, which consisted of two rooms hewn into rock, which were covered with grey hydraulic plaster to make them watertight. Upon excavation, this building showed signs of violent destruction.

Remains of a Roman hot-bath-house, of the hypocaust style, were excavated to the East of the synagogue. Scant attention has been paid to this installation, which is unfortunate as the social impact of this Roman institution amid an observant community (if this is indeed Modein) is significant and suggests a lessoning of strict Jewish values under Herod. Certainly Herod himself favoured a hot-bath and built eleven bathhouses in his five palaces: one in his fortress, Machaerus, and two or three in each of his other palaces.[24]

The *mikvah* at Modi'in was constructed in the Herodian or third phase of the synagogue, perhaps, perhaps because a Roman hot bath-house would not have been acceptable without it because a public bath-house was, of itself, defiling and an immediate ritual immersion was required after its use.

Why? Perhaps because users had urinated in the water (or worse), gentiles and the impure may use the facility and public nudity was unseemly. Also statues of idols and paintings of human figures and naked goddesses were the usual decorations in bath-houses.[25] The *Mishnah* of c.200 C.E. provides another insight. Discussions and religious contemplation were forbidden in bath-houses:[26] presumably because Jews were not to loiter in the nude there, perhaps because of temptation and because it was an unseemly place for thoughts about God and observant Jews scrupulously avoided deliberate contamination.

Roman bathhouses were associated with status and Hellenism. Modein was the hometown of three Maccabean high priests and they were buried there in a magnificent marble mausoleum so the town may have reflected the fashionable trends of the priestly class. Public bathhouses were rarely found out in the communities but rooms provided with a *hypercaust* were fashionable amongst the priests and the wealthy. Every house in the Upper City of Jerusalem had one or more *mikvah'ot* and many also had a *caldarium*. [27] Privacy, and proximity to their own *mikvah*, would have overcome any problems of *halakhot* (Jewish laws) and the decorations would have been appropriate and modest.

The ancient village surrounding the synagogue at Modi'in was a small agricultural settlement, set amongst olive trees and grapevines. It prospered during the Hellenistic and Early Roman Periods. The site was excavated c.2010 under Alexander Onn and Shlomit Weksler-Bdolah, who identified it as ancient Modein. [28] A hill above Modi'in is currently being excavated in the search for the Maccabee family's marble mausoleum but Boaz Zissu and others believe that the burial site of the Maccabees has already been found and they challenge the identification (by the excavators Onn and Weksler-Bdolah) of the village around Umm el-'Umdan as Modein. [29]

The thought of finding evidence of the dramatic mausoleum attracts interest as it was built by Simon, ruler and high priest, the last son of Mattathias to survive and who was very popular with the people. It was described by Josephus as of brilliantly white marble, tall, with pillars and porticos. Its seven towers (five for the sons and two larger ones for their parents) could be seen from a long distance. [30] Because of the high status of the Maccabees and the magnificence of the building it would have been a 1st-century equivalent of a tourist attraction and was in the vicinity of Emmaus, where Jesus' close relatives lived. [31]

The writer Hegessipus identified Cleopas/Clopas of Emmaus as Joseph's brother and the Holy Family was certainly close to him and to Mary-Clopas. (This Clopas was identified by the historian Eusebius as the father of Simon/Symeon).[32] Mary-Clopas joined Jesus' mother, Mary, her sister Salome, and Mary Magdalene at the crucifixion (Jn. 19:25).[33] If, during the many years of his youth or young adulthood, Jesus ever visited his relatives in Emmaus (an easy 7 miles/11km walk from Jerusalem [Lk. 24:13-15])[34] he would have glimpsed (or visited) the mausoleum and probably have seen this large synagogue (Plate 1.B.).[35]

1.3. Kiryat Sefer

Kiryat Sefer is only 16km (10 miles) north of Modi'in. In the 1st century C.E. it was a very small village. In the centre of the ancient village square a small 1st-century synagogue of the 'Galilee style' was excavated in the late 1990's by Y. Magen.[36]

The building is unusual because of its unique plan and its position in the centre of the village.[37] Its roof was supported by four free-standing Doric-style columns and four pilasters attached to the front and back walls.

The ancient village is remarkable in that each house had an inner courtyard and its own private *mikvah* to ensure the constant purity of workers who made kosher wine and oil, perhaps for priestly homes and/ or for the Temple.

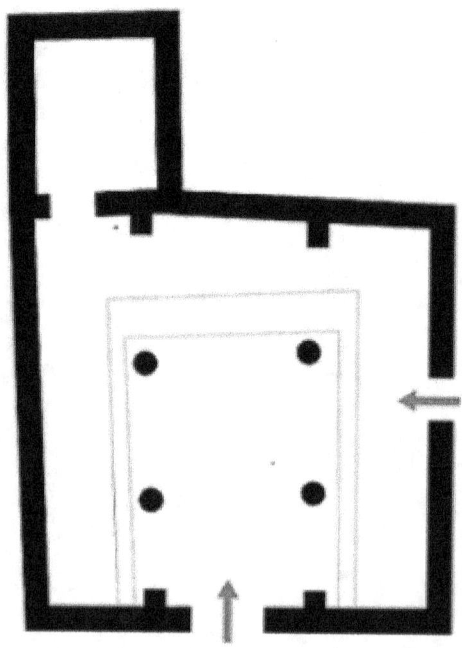

**Plate 1.C. Kiryat Sefer synagogue,
Design Dept., Shofarot Publications.**

Some homes were found with olive presses and mills for grinding flour. Coin hoards from the 3rd-to-2nd-century BCE, which contained many gold coins, attest to the prosperity of the village. The excessive number of make-up palettes discovered suggests that money was available and that the women were very conscious of their appearance;[38] all indications of affluence. A rare juglett, with elaborate decoration but careless craftsmanship, represents the work of a local glassblower.[39]

1.4. Horvat 'Ethri

In 1999 excavation work on a small but well-planned village in the Bet Shemesh area 35km/c.21 miles S-W of Jerusalem was commenced under Boaz Zissu.

**Plate 1.D. Plan of M1 at Horvat 'Ethri.
Design Dept., Shofarot Publications.**

Once known as 'Hoah', it is now officially named Horvat 'Ethri (from an *ostracon* marked 'Ethri'). The site, on a spur commanding an expansive view, was first settled in the 4th century B.C.E. but the majority of the numismatic and pottery evidence dates from the 1st century B.C.E. This was the high point of village expansion here - and therefore of its population and wealth, and a favourable time for large construction projects. Horvat 'Ethri was partially destroyed in 69 C.E. and was only partly reoccupied afterwards, until the Bar Kokhba war of 132-134 C.E. It was briefly occupied by retired Roman veterans but was deserted after 200 C.E.[40] This pattern has been seen elsewhere: settlements that struggled to survive the first destruction, in 70 C.E., were deserted after the second revolt. There is real evidence of Roman destruction of even small villages across The Land.[41]

In parts of Horvat 'Ethri, a layer of ash and burnt wood was found, with human remains and in one *mikvah* 7 adults and 4 adolescents and a fetus had been buried together. One had been beheaded.[42]

The ruin of Horvat 'Ethri was rich in artefacts: a stone well-mouth, pottery and glass, oil lamps, stone vessels such as priests used, a balista stone, grinding stones, four wine-presses and coins from as early as the Late Ptolemaic (c.250-166 B.C.E.) and the Hasmonaean (167-63 B.C.E.) periods. Some houses had underground basements and beneath the surface a honeycomb of inter-connecting tunnels, hiding places, wells, cisterns and burial caves had been laboriously dug in the bedrock.

A 'broadhouse-style' building called M1, constructed with very large stones (75cm x 50cm or 2'6" by 1'8") has survived in part to a height of 1.5m/c.5'. It was set within a courtyard. Two massive stone column-bases indicate that the roof had been supported by three columns. M1 was a substantial and important building although it lacks the customary stone stepped benches, which facilitate buildings being identified as synagogues but such stones may have been removed for reuse later. It did, however have three *mikvah'ot* close by. The presence in the village of at least four *mikvah'ot* suggests a very pious community which would have needed a synagogue, furthermore, architectural elements (Doric-style capitals, as at Kiryat Sefer, and moulded cornices) suggest that it was a synagogue at one stage, perhaps with portable wooden furniture. Much labour was expended on this building as it was constructed with a stone rubble core between two layers of dressed stone blocks facing internally and externally: a major undertaking as these walls were .9m (c.3') thick. In overall size M1 is smaller than Umm el-Umdan, but only by about two square metres. It has not been definitely dated and may have post-dated 'the Jesus period'.[43]

Strangely, the intact domestic buildings of Horvat 'Ethri were not reoccupied after 69 C.E.: only the burnt section of the village was reinhabited and rebuilt after the Roman attack and the rebuilding of the accommodation would have been the immediate priority, rather than construction of a large public building. Perhaps houses were left vacant for returnees who never came back. Or perhaps the fire burnt any bodies and/or purified the destroyed sections so that they could be rebuilt and reused. Construction would have been difficult after 70 C.E. because of shortages of skilled manpower, population and probably finances. No other, similar building in Israel has been dated to the period between the Roman wars.

Of the four *mikva'ot* found, some date from the Hasmonaean period,[44] including one in the vestibule of building M1 and a larger one in an enclosed structure close to its entrance. Rainwater from courtyards and plazas was channelled into these, facilitated by the careful placement of the buildings.[45] This demonstrates that the community followed the religious tradition of using 'water from Heaven' for ritual purification.

Although identification of the main building at Horvat 'Ethri as a synagogue is problematic it resembles those of Kiryat Sefer and Modi'in and may have been a transitional building towards a synagogue of the broad-house style, as its door was on the long wall.

Remnants of numerous pre-destruction synagogues have been found in Israel. Newly discovered synagogues provide an ever-growing body of evidence to excite academic study and they support the New Testament's claim that synagogues were widespread.

1.5. Massada

Even as recently as 1960 the noted archaeologist William Albright had written that there were no Roman-period synagogues in Israel save for the Theodotus inscription.[46] The breakthrough came soon afterwards: in 1964. On Herod's fortress of Massada overlooking the Dead Sea, amid great excitement the flamboyant Israeli archaeologist, Yigael Yadin, son of archaeologist E. L. Sukenik, discovered a pre-destruction synagogue (Plate 1.E) with its nearby triple-pooled *mikvah* for ritual purification (Plate 1.F.). Yadin immediately announced his find as a mikvah, which was soon confirmed my eminent rabbis. [47]

Plate 1.E. Synagogue, Massada.
Photo: D. Campbell, 1994.

A small room, which had previously housed animals, had been converted for use as a synagogue in about 68 C.E.[48] It was only used until 73 C.E. when Massada fell to the Roman attackers. In stage two of its creation, a chamber had been walled off in the back corner, presumably for storage. Remnants of Scriptural scrolls were unearthed in this enclosure, which strongly suggests that Bible reading took place there. An ostracon inscribed "*priestly tithe*" was found on the floor, adding a further hint.[49]

Massada's destruction by the Romans in 73 C.E. clearly dates this example to the 1st-century C.E.

Mikvah'ot on Massada

Because ritual purity as not required for meetings other than those of a sacred, one might say 'religious', nature, it would be pointless to construct a *mikvah* beside a large public building that had no cultic or sacred purpose. Thus the proximity of a *mikvah* is extremely important for identifying early synagogues.[50] This is not to say that synagogues were never used for secular purposes: but Jews did not distinguish sacred from secular as Westerners do.

Since Yadin excavated Massada it has been believed that there were different levels of purity, which influenced the construction of any particular *mikvah*, but with some disagreement about whether the Pharisees or the Sadducees practised the higher level of purity.

Recently, however this distinction has been called into question (for example by Yonatan Adler)[51] and the matter is still under consideration in scholarship.

It is known, however, that flowing water and the ocean provided the highest level of purification. There was not a 'one size fits all' standard of levels of purity, for example a *mikvah* or body of water a certain distance out into the country, sufficed for a man but not for female monthly purification, but the same pool further away from town might suffice for both. A pool that is near a town or a road would not adequate because people might wash in it.[52]

**Plate 1.F. Configuration of three pools, Massada.
Photograph: Ian Finnin, 2018.**

Just outside the Temple Mount, single pools were the norm, but they were all filled by 'water from heaven', that is, rainwater that was channelled down from Temple Mount without human intervention, so these pools fulfilled the requirements for 'living water'. Similarly, up on Massada, the rainwater was carefully collected and channelled into underground cisterns or the *mikvah'ot*. It is said that enough food and water was stored up there to outlast a ten-year siege.

There is currently considerable controversy about the proposed use of an *otzer/ozer* or reserve pool of 'living water' so the exact purpose for the three pools at Massada is uncertain. The small pool on the extreme left in Plate 1.F may have been for washing the dust off hands or feet before immersion.[53] Only one pool had steps down. A plastered water conduit lead rainwater between the two larger tanks, one of which was too small for immersion and may only been a reservoir but neither more nor less purifying than the other pool, as Adler contends.[54]

All *mikvah'ot* were probably both covered and enclosed - for privacy, to prevent insects and animals contaminating it by drowning in it, and to discourage the growth of algae, which is stimulated by sunlight.[55]

The synagogue at Massada is typical of others from the period, which were found subsequently and called 'Galilee Style'. Such synagogues were square or rectangular in shape, with banks of stone seats built-in around three or four sides and with any number of stone central columns to hold up the roof span. The congregants faced inwards.

Detail of Plate 1F.

This detail clerarly shows which pool was the *tevilah*. It also shows two sets of stairs, one bottom centre for easy access and another to the right. This mikvah complex abbouts gthe outer wall of Massada and efenders on the wall could enter the water at that point.

1.6. Synagogue of Herodium

About a decade after Yadin's important discovery on Massada, a dining room that had been converted into a synagogue was discovered on Herodium, which was Herod's fortress on a man-made hill, near Bethlehem (Plate 1.G.). One cannot, however, claim that either or both synagogues were built under royal patronage as Herod the Great, who had built both fortresses, was long dead before the pious Jewish rebels occupied both sites.[56]

"Netzer conclusively shows that Herod built a synagogue neither at Massada nor at any other of his palaces or fortresses".[57]

Plate 1.G. *Mikvah* **and synagogue on Herodium.**
Photograph: Ian Finnin, 2018.

In particular the Massada synagogue, was small and rough-and-ready. Like it, the synagogue on Herodium, and its adjacent *mikvah* had also been constructed in about 67/68 C.E. shortly before the Roman army finally conquered the Holy Land: that is, decades after both Herod's period and 'the Jesus Period'.[58]

There are four mikva'ot on Herodium: two near the dining-room cum synagogue, built by the rebels who made the conversion, and two internally, presumably built by Herod. Not that Herod was observant of Judaism but he liked to be seen that way by his subjects and he spared no expense to provide every facility for his guests, who were both Jewish and pagan, The synagogue is currently roofed over but Herod's triclinium (dining-room) was longer and included the columns visible to the rear of Plate 1.G.

Bolstered by Lee I. Levine's work of 2005,[59] students of the origins of the synagogue have hastened to adopt the view that the 1st-century C.E. buildings (such as those just listed) were used as much for 'secular' as 'religious' purposes. Some even believe that 'secular' usage preceded 'sacred'[60] and/or was more important.[61] Many scholars believe that village synagogues had many civic uses, which could include education, local administration and as law courts for local disputes.[62]

It may be the case that education (probably of boys and men) was the primary purpose of the synagogue, certainly some scholars consider educational usage to have been *"of basic importance"*.[63] The evidence (both literary and archaeological) is scant and scattered for claims for social and political activities in synagogues.[64]

Perhaps praise, worship and/or prayer did not usually occur there in the 1st century, as there is minimal record of them, except for Josephus' reference to a large *proseuche* (a prayer-house) in Tiberius (*Life* 54-66).[65] The only meetings there that he notes, however, were political in nature, except that one Monday morning Josephus tried to say private prayers there until he was interrupted.[66] This is a hint, but hardly conclusive evidence.

The fact the Jesus and his disciples sang a hymn at the Last Supper (Mk.14:26; Mt. 26:30) and that the singing of psalms, hymns and spiritual songs was a very early Christian practice (Eph. 5:19, Col. 3:15) suggests that congregational singing was typical in Judaism. Paul and Silas sang hymns together while imprisoned (Acts 16:25) praises that they both seem to have known. This suggests that a commonly-known Jewish repertoire of songs of praise existed.

1.7. Was there a Synagogue at Khirbet Qumran beside the Dead Sea?

Put simply, the answer is Yes and No.

No because there was no designated, separate building used as a synagogue. They didn't need one because they regarded their twice-daily communal meal as their holy place, their sacred space and the food of the initiated members was called the pure Meal of the Congregation (4Q265, fragment 1). This is why, before they ate, they each purified themselves in one of their many *mikvah'ot* and put on clean clothing, just as if they were going onto Temple Mount.

The various Dead Sea Scrolls that deal with the rules of the community tell us that their dining room was also their civic assembly hall in which matters of organization and administration were discussed and voted upon.[67]

The Refectory or dining room in Plate 1H is the longest room at Khirbet Qumran, was also their schoolroom in which the Scriptures were expounded every night. Professor Lawrence Schiffman offers the following references for this:[68] there was reading every night to expound the Mosaic Law (*Community Rule* [*CR*] 6:7-8); Bible study (*CR* 7:1); expounding and reading the book on the Sabbath (4Q *hab* 251.1:5);

perhaps private study,[69] listening to the priests, who read clearly and audibly ("*lest he cause error in a capital manner*").[70]

Although with different emphases and a different flavour, this all parallels what took place in the synagogues of Jewish communities all over Israel: Scriptural instruction, civic gathering and eating together. So yes, there was a synagogue at Qumran. It was a multi-purpose room, with no built-in stone seating, but at the very heart of the community.

Plate 1.H. The Refectory at Qumran. Public domain.

1.8. Conclusions

The two synagogues established by the rebels on Massada and Herodium naturally form a different category from the three found in Judean villages. For one thing they were not purpose-built as synagogues: the one on Massada previously housed animals and that on Herodium had been a dining room. The criticism that they lacked a niche for Torah scrolls may be anachronistic or the result of necessity. A scroll-fragment was found buried in the floor at Massada but can we be sure the rebels even possessed scrolls?

Each category has more in common within its category than between categories. Together, however, they indicate a high degree of Jewish observance, demonstrated by the presence of stone vessels, multiple *mikva'ot,* careful conservation of *'living water'* and the size, centrality and careful construction of each of the buildings that were probably used for Torah-teaching.

Qumran was a unique example. It was an Essene-like community but may not have been exactly the same so that conclusions drawn from what (little) is known about the Essenes in Jerusalem or Ein-Gedi, for example, may not have been applicable.

Umm el-Umdan, Kiryat Sefer and the lost synagogue of Theodotus may be the oldest synagogues known of in Israel so far and they are not in Galilee but in Judea and not far from the Temple in Jerusalem, which was their contemporary.

Chapter 2
First-Century Synagogues in Galilee

Texts such as Acts 6:9, indicate that there were a variety of synagogues in Jerusalem, such as the Synagogue of the Freedmen (Libertines) which included freed slaves from Cyrenia and Alexandria and perhaps another for those from Cilicia and Asia. The New Testament suggests that synagogues in Jerusalem were based upon members' social class, language or geographic origin, as was certainly the case in Rome, about which a lot has been learned.

Even very early there was a distinction in Jerusalem (based upon ethnicity) between 'Hebrews' and 'Hellenists' among Jesus' followers (Acts 6:1). Villages in Galilee, however, were more homogeneous than either Rome or Jerusalem, with local marriages being common and extended families being close. A sense of community would have been facilitated by water-transport from village to village around the Lake.

2.1. Capernaum

Capernaum, the epicenter of 'the Jesus ministry' and virtually all tour groups visit the beautiful remains of the white limestone synagogue: but it is dated to the Byzantine Period. Few look at the basalt foundations although they have their own, more significant, story to tell.

These basalt walls protrude on all sides, both outside and inside the limestone synagogue building above (vivible in Plate 2.B). It was once a massive public building: roughly constructed by comparison with the white, Byzantine-era synagogue, but larger. Not only that but it had rows of columns supported by walls that were exactly beneath the interior columns of the limestone building. That is, the wide strong walls and stylobates that supported the 1st century columns are still supporting the 4th century columns.

These walls are generally accepted as those built and financed by the Roman centurion who met Jesus, as recorded in Luke 7:5.[71] This would have been expensive to b build as it would have been greater in area than any other known synagogue in Israel: greater than the limestone synagogue and also greater than Galma.

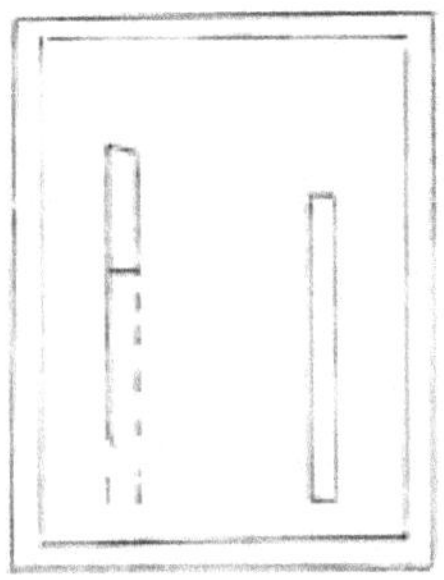

Plate 2.A. Capernaum.
Plan of 1st century basalt walls.
Design Dept., Shofarot Publications.

**Plate 2.B. Basalt wall beneath limestone wall.
Photograph: Ian Finnin, 2018.**

2.2. Gamla

This synagogue is in the destroyed town of Gamla in the Golan Heights, above and overlooking the Lake of Galilee. The Jewish historian, Josephus, as commander of Jewish forces in the Galilee, supervised Gamla's fortification and was, perhaps, an eye-witness to its ruin as he described how Gamla fell to the Roman invaders in 67 C.E.

The textual evidence of his history, *War of the Jews*,[72] dovetails with what the archaeologists eventually found.

Gamla lay in the Golan Heights, untouched for almost 2,000 years. The synagogue, in Plate 2.C., pre-dates the Common Era and may date from the first century B.C.E.

Plate 2.C. Gamla Synagogue. Public domain.

There is much interest in the question of whether an upper storey was (or contained) a gallery for women. A temporary separation barrier between men and women may have been used (canes or rugs have been suggested) even in small, early, single-storey synagogues, but that fact is not spelt out as early as the 1st century C.E. The Babylonian Talmud, a late source (*bt.Sukkot* 51b-52b) however, suggests the use of a *mechitza* or dividing wall, as noted by the Egyptian Jewish philosopher, Philo, in the communal hall of the Therapeutae sect in Egypt. Perhaps, however, gender-separation was not a major issue, or more probably, women did not attend public synagogues, which Philo regarded as right and proper, although they were not forbidden. Philo assumes that (in Egypt at least) ideally women did not attend synagogue but were concerned only with the household and he noted that they occupied the rear section of houses there, although Egyptian praxis might not have been typical of Israel. The discussions of the issue of a gallery in the *Mishnah* and *Talmud* (*Niddah.* 2:5, *m.Sukkah* 5:1-4 and *bt.Sukkah* 4:1) are of limited application, being later, but they confirm a separation, although this may not have applied in the 1st-century C.E. A stair tread was found among other items in secondary use at Gvamla. This suggests that the first building on the site was two storeys high, as indeed this stage may also have been as it had at least eighteen columns and so was suitable for a second storey. It is a basalt rectangular building of 'dry wall' construction and, being 22m x 17m (72' x c.56'), it is the largest building in the town so far excavated (although 90% of the city remains buried).

At Gamla, an *exedra* (a small room) at the front (about 25' 7" x 8' 2", or 7.8m x 2.5m) [a total of 19.5 sq. metres or 209 sq. ft.] was interpreted as a space for women: if so, very few women and small children were expected to attend - especially as the main hall may have seated between perhaps 300 and 430 people.

A small room at the rear of the synagogue, 3.5 x 5.6m (about 11' 6" x 18' 4"|), had stone bench seating on all sides and a window, which opened into the main hall. The room was probably used for education and the rabbi, through the window, could observe the students.

There is no doubt that Gamla was destroyed in c.68 C.E. and not reinhabited. Its 'Galilee style' synagogue so closely resembles others of the period that scepticism is not appropriate.

Ritual baths *(Mikvah'ot)* at Gamla

There is a *mikvah* close to the Gamla synagogue's main entrance, one of four so far found in that city, which show that the inhabitants observed the requirements for ritual purity. Appropriately, two of these *mikva'ot* were found in an olive oil factory, demonstrating the need for agricultural workers to immerse.[73]

Plate 2.D. *Mikvah* with steps. Photo: Justin Campbell, 2019.

2.3. Magdala/Migdal

In 2009, a 1st-century synagogue was discovered in Tarichaea (also called both Magdala and Migdal). Before 70 C.E., this town was substantial and prosperous, with a flourishing trade in the catching, drying and salting of fish, the staple protein of ordinary folk. It had an artificial harbour for more than 200 boats of a particular style known to us from an ancient mosaic depiction found at Magdala and from the salvaged and preserved example on display in Kibbutz Nof Ginnosar. The town of Magdala is currently being excavated and closely examined for clues about the history of life in Galilee in the pre-destruction period.

Magdala was built with a main street crossed at right angles (as in the Roman manner). It had a residential area where the floors were earthen, a wealthier area with some stone or mosaic floors and some two-storey houses and also a 'religious quarter' with indications of Jewish praxis: four *mikvah'ot*, a shovel for ash and stone vessels such as priests used. There were grain-storage buildings with paved stone floors and also bread ovens and flourmills. A large basalt bowl was set up at the entrance to the synagogue: probably a water-bowl for the washing of hands (as also found at the Ostia synagogue).

About 2,400 coins have been found. One vital example found in the central floor area of the synagogue was minted in nearby Tiberius in the time of Herod the Tetrarch, in 29 C.E: within the 'Jesus period'. The building was commenced between 5 and 10 C.E. but expanded in c.40 C.E. to seat more people. It was abandoned as the Roman army approached in c.67 C.E. and some of its stones and columns were reused to build defensive barricades across the streets so its pre-destruction date is hardly ever contested.

The battle for Magdala was bloody and furious. Josephus had recorded the last hours of the town after a fierce naval battle on the lake fought by fishing boats (War III.10.1-5) against Roman rafts. Although he was given to exaggeration, Joseph wrote that the battle for Magdala left 6,500 dead (War II. 10-9f). Vespasian then killed the old people, took 30,400 into slavery and sent 6,000 young men to the Emperor Nero and some to King Agrippa to be sold as slaves by them.

The synagogue may have been the home-synagogue of Mary Magdalene, who was so close to Jesus that some have theorised that they were married and he did entrust her with the task of telling the disciples of his resurrection.

Because it was close to the Sea of Galilee, those disciples who were fishermen would certainly have seen and heard it being constructed when they were out fishing on the lake. It is reasonable to suppose that, when Jesus lived at Capernaum on the North side of the Lake of Galilee, he would have passed through Magdala, which was on the *Via Maris*, the main route from Nazareth to Capernaum.

Jesus and some of his disciples may even have briefly attended this synagogue. It would clearly have been one of the synagogues in which Jesus preached as he went all over Galilee to preach. The twelve apostles *"went from village to village, preaching the gospel and healing people everywhere"* (Lk. 9:6). In preparation for Jesus' visits the seventy-two went ahead of him *"to every town and place where he was about to go"* (Lk.10:1) so it seems that Magdala received intense spiritual ministry. No wonder the synagogue had to be enlarged.

Plate 2.E. Overview of Magdala synagogue.
This image was kindly provided by the Magdala Project

It is reasonable to suppose that, when Jesus lived at Capernaum on the North side of the lake, he would have passed through Magdala as it was on the *Via Maris*, the main route from Nazareth to Capernaum.

Jesus and some of his disciples may even have briefly attended this very synagogue.

At Magdala synagogue, the long vestibule or entrance hall had a low bench along one wall and it may have served as a space for education (a *Beit Midrash*). There was a rectangular chalkstone there, in secondary use, which may have served as a table for scrolls (visible in Plate 2.E). Note also the white patch of flooring nearby. This a small room with its mosaic floor and painted walls may have been used for scroll-storage (the *Aron HaKadosh*).[74] Other small rooms nearby may have been used for hospitality or for storing the Temple taxes. The study-room leads into the main hall or reading room (Plate 2.E.), which is almost square with one doorway and an ambulatory all around (behind the columns). This architecture facilitated the accessing of seats without crossing the pebble-covered central space, which may have been carpeted.

Plate 2.F. A painted wall at Magdala.
Photo: Justin Campbell. 2018.

The ambulatory was paved with incomplete black and white mosaics in a meander pattern. Its completed section features a rosette, a symbol that was often used on Jewish ossuaries of the 1st century, and in synagogues.

This same pattern also decorates the mosaic floor of a nearby house, which also has two rows of stone benches, as if meetings were held there. The exact meaning of this symbol is obscure, but the simple rosette was a premier 'religious' symbol in the 1st century and was found on a lintel of the Gamla synagogue and above the entrance of the Kiryat Sefer synagogue. A rosette was also found in Jerusalem, in the debris, in the same cistern as the Theodotus inscription (illustrated in Plate 1.A.) and must have decorated that synagogue.

Internally, in its last phase at least, the walls at Magdala were plastered and then painted in five colours (red, mustard yellow and blue panels set within rectangular frames of black and white) so the interior would have been very colourful (Plate 2.E.). All congregants faced inwards but some, perhaps, sat in the central floor area on carpets.

Plate 2.G. Magdala: synagogue hall.
Photograph: Ian Finnin, 2018.

The building did not face the lake, nor Jerusalem, but the street. Typically, the most convenient orientation for each building was characteristic of the early 'Galilee style'.

Internally the Magdala main hall has the usual banks of seats around all four sides. With only six stone columns to support the roof a second storey is unlikely but the central section may have been raised to allow for clerestory windows to provide light into the interior. Debris from the collapsed ceiling indicated that it was made of wooden beams and mortar and coated on the inside with white plaster. Although it was built in basalt, a very dark stone, its interior would have been light and colourful.

Plate 2.Ha.The Magdala stone in situ,
Photo: Justin Campbell, 2019.

This Magdala synagogue is unique for the period because, on the floor of the hall, a carved limestone block was found, which may have been the base of a lecturn. Its carved images include an unmistakable Jewish symbol, a menorah. Five faces of the stone are carved but the meanings of the symbols is a challenge after 2,000 years.

The excavators, and Richard Bauckham and others have formed interpretations, but even the identity of each item is subject to conjecture. For example on its top two matching items have been viewed as both date-palm trees and rakes used to scrape ash and burnt bones from the Altar of Sacrifice in the Temple. Similarly, the hanging circular objects on both of the long sides (visible in Plate 2.Ha) have been interpreted variously as incense shovels, censers and oil lamps.

Plate 2.Hb. End of the Magdala stone.

Photo: Ian Finnin, 2018.

As the Table of Shewbread with its twelve loaves was often regarded as the most important of the three items of furniture in the Holy Place and because the main feature of the face of the stone is a rosette-with-twelve-petals, the stone is easily associated the Table of Shewbread. Initially the rosette was thought to represent the twelve loaves of shewbread offered weekly in the Temple, or the twelve months of the celestial year. We suggest an eschatological meaning: that the twelve petals represent the whole house of Israel: all twelve tribes, in the midst of the Temple. Interestingly, Richard Bauckham offers a similar solution by interpreting the rear symbols (those in Plate 2.Hb) with Ez.24:1-9 in mind. This combination results in an important and personal meaning for the congregation assembled together: that the Divine presence is with them as they meet; just as if they were in the Temple. The iconography of the rosette on the top, with its twelve petals (or rosette-within-a-circle)

motif is connected to the 1st century Temple as a mosaic example of this symbol has been found in the burnt-out mansion of a priest in the Upper City of Jerusalem.

The iconography found within the Magdala synagogue is complex but it includes three important Jewish symbols found elsewhere: the simple rosette, the Menorah and the circle-composed-of-twelve-petals.

The Magdala synagogue challenges much 20th century scholarship because of its demonstrable relationship to the Jewish cult and Temple and the early use of Jewish iconography: the Menorah, the rosette and the twelve-petal flower motif. The façade of the stone shown in Plate 2.Hc features two columns, two amphorae and a Menorah on what may be a pedestal or the entrance to the Temple, with its characteristic curtains parted.

**Plate 2Hc. Magdala Stone front.
Kindly provided by the Magdala Project.**

In the street, at the entrance to the synagogue, there is a basalt basin in situ, probably for the washing of hands. It is further evidence for the growing custom of hand-washing before reading the Scriptures, praying or eating, as noted in Mark 7:5 and in the discussion of the Khirbet Cana synagogue, below.

Conclusions About the Magdala Synagogue

Magdala Synagogue can be regarded as the epicentre of Judeo-Christian archaeology. It is of great value as it is from the 'Jesus period', is in the heart of Galilee and is situated on the half-way point between Nazareth and Capernaum on the *Via Maris*, a route Jesus would have travelled. Perhaps it is as close as modern people have yet come to Jesus, and is more personal than the basalt building at Capernaum, which was probably built by the Roman centurion, because the Magdala synagogue can still be entered.

From a practical point of view the Magdala example illustrates many aspects of synagogue construction typical of the period in size, internal arrangement, shape, seating, and study room. Its uniqueness stems from the typically Jewish iconography of the carved stone found in situ, which highlights the sacred use for the synagogue.

"The stone symbolises a cultic connection between the synagogue and the Temple. It is unique evidence of the way Galilean Jews before 70 understood the synagogue and its activities".[75]

2.4. Khirbet Cana

The synagogue at Khirbet Cana (a ruined village that is not to be confused with Kfar Cana) was built on top of a hill above a fertile valley, sixteen kilometres due west of Magdala. The synagogue was large, but slightly smaller than that at Gamla, being 20x15m internally (65' 7" x 49' 3"). It was certainly a substantial, public building because the walls were 1.5m thick. This building was huge for such a small village, suggesting a high degree of commitment and probably of Jewish observance and of economic prosperity.

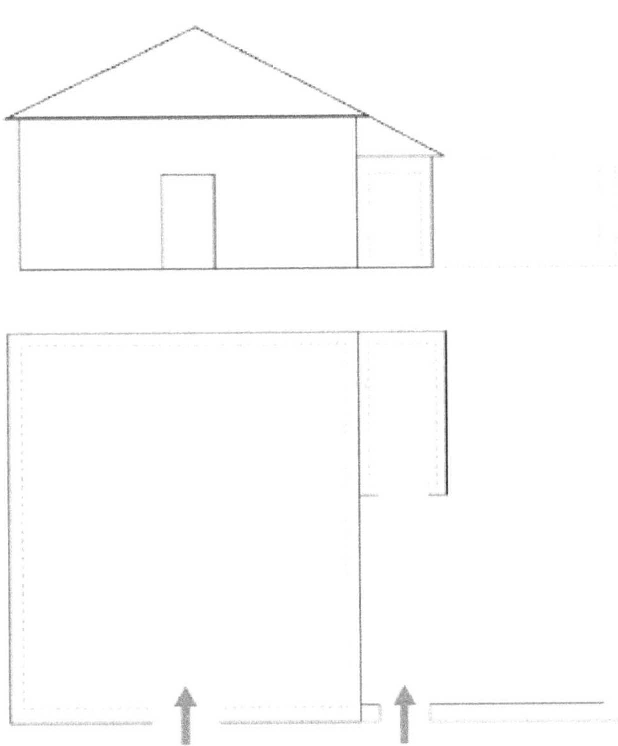

Plate 2J. Khirbet Cana
Design Depart., Shofarot Publications.

In John 2:6, Cana of Galilee was the site of Jesus' first miracle (turning water into wine) and the huge, full stone water-jars were ready for the washing of hands and feet. The event was possibly a family wedding because Mary played such a prominent role. She was a family, even a village, matriarch. Jesus and six disciples were guests and Cana was the hometown of the disciple, Nathaniel, who may have been somehow related to the married couple, or even to Mary and Jesus.

The social setting suggests an observant Jewish community in which ritual purity was observed. Even in Old Testament times Cana had been the home of the priestly family of Eliashib as one of the 24 orders of *Cohanim* who ministered in the Temple (I Chron. 24:19).

Between 1997 and 2008 the excavation of Khirbet Cana was led by Douglas Edwards and then by Tom McCullough whose main interest was in demonstrating that the site was the original 'Cana of Galilee'. Dating the synagogue was a secondary concern but they were able to date it by pottery to 'Hellenistic' or 'early Roman' periods and by Carbon 14 to 4 to 235 C.E. It seems that it could not, however, have been built (nor completed) in the late-first-to-early-second century as the population and the economy of Israel's North were destroyed by the Romans in 67 C.E. and would not have recovered so quickly (except that some towns, such as Zippori/Sepphoris, were spared by quickly surrendering to the Romans). Many skilled workers and labourers in the North would have been killed. Stone for the project was quarried in various sites but mainly at the Horns of Hittin, near Tiberius, about 15km/9.3 miles away, so transport would have been a logistical problem, especially during a time of poverty and/or devastation.

Since being excavated the site has been totally neglected. Access is difficult and thorn bushes have grown around and about. Neither the Franciscan Order, which controls Catholic sites on behalf of the Papacy, nor the Israeli government seem interested in opening it to the public. The Magdalla synagogue may have suffered the same fate, but for the unique Magdala Stone, the site's proximity to habitation and the vision of one man, Father Juan Maria Solanda. Israel has so many Biblical sites requiring excavation and preservation, but this one should demand the attention of Christians, even though the Catholic Church is invested in Kfar Cana..

The Khirbet Cana building had one adjacent small room (3x4m/9' 10" x 13' 1") which was entered via the courtyard; as noted in the drawn plan (Plate 2.H.). This room had stone benches on three sides for seating and may have been used as a meeting room for small groups, or as a classroom, or both.

The presence of a *mikvah* beside the entrance here at Khirbet Cana, as at Gamla, along with their interior arrangements, help to identify them as synagogues and attest to the respect in which each community held their synagogue. Their insistence upon at least one ritual-immersion-pool indicates that use of the building was not entirely 'secular' or, at the very least, that the community observed female 'domestic purity', which, according to the *Mishnah,* was a community's first priority.

2.5. Tel Rechesh

In 2016, in Galilee near Mt Tabor, a small, early synagogue was unearthed. The dig, which was led by Mordechai (Moti) Aviam,[76] found a building 26ft by 29.5 ft (7.9m by 9m). It has two banks of limestone seating, made of beautiful white Ashlar stones,[77] and the remains of one of the two column bases, which once supported the roof span. Some of the flooring is intact. This synagogue was more than a Sabbath day's walk from any previously known village and was probably built by the estate owners for their families and farm-workers. It provides added confirmation of the New Testament's assertion that, in the Roman period, there were synagogues throughout Galilee: even, apparently, in unexpected places. The site survived the Great Revolt intact (c.67) but was abandoned after the Bar Kokhba Revolt.

2.6. Shuafat (Khirbet a-Ras)

At Shuafat, a 1st century B.C.E. ruin was recently discovered, which numerous scholars identify as a synagogue. It had a *mikvah* but it is still poorly published and some scholars are doubtful.[78] It was set in an agricultural complex. As at Gamla and Kiryat Sefer, agricultural workers had to be scrupulous about ritual purity, so its *mikvah* may not necessarily be supporting evidence for a synagogue in such a setting. (Perhaps the *mikvah* was provided for the workers, not worshipers.) The similarly small example at Tel Rechesh (above) adds weight to a positive identification of Shuafat as a synagogue. Other than being possible evidence for another synagogue in a remote location, the main interest of Khirbet a-Ras/Shuafat lies in the fact that the main floor is divided by a low wall (as was added to the hall at Hamat Tiberius in the 4th century or later). Shuafat is the oldest suggestion of possible gender separation, but is not conclusive.[79]

2.7. A Recent Discovery in Zippori/Sepphoris

In 2016, a large public building erected on earlier remains and with coloured frescoes of human and animal figures was discovered in Zippori by The Hebrew University of Jerusalem, led by Zeev Weiss. In its publicity the University states that among the many monumental finds in Zippori is a 1st-century synagogue,[80] although others are more cautious about its identification.[81]

Zippori's monuments had more chance of survival because it escaped destruction in 67 C.E. as it was loyal to Rome, perhaps remembering that Rome had destroyed the rebellious city after the death of King Herod in 4 B.C.E. It was rewarded for its loyalty with the status of a 'polis.'[82]

which included taxation benefits. After the second revolt against Rome it was renamed Diocaesarea in honour of Zeus and Caesar. The Sanhedrin met there and Judah ha-Nasi edited the *Mishnah* there.[83]

The Jerusalem Talmud of the 5th century identified 18 synagogues in Zippori (jTal. 9:4, 3 b). Now scholars identify two ancient synagogues but neither is as early as the 1st-century. One, discovered in c.1994 has amazing mosaics and inscriptions in Greek, Hebrew and Aramaic and is dated 5th to 6th century. In fact amazing mosaics are characteristic of Zippori and include the Nilotic House, the Dionysus Villa and the synagogue. The huge water reservoir is also amazing. There are over 60 *mikvah'ot* in Zippori, but the proportion of Jews to gentiles in the city has long been a matter of scholarly contention.[84]

Although still controversial, by the time this book is read there might be a more remains of the other 16 ancient synagogues found.

2.8. A Second Synagogue at Magdala

Magdala has the distinction of being the only town so far known to boast two separate 1st-century synagogues. Recently discovered, a small, plain, white plastered synagogue has been unearthed in the industrial part of the town where the fish were processed.

Chapter 3
Overall Conclusions

(1) Conclusions About 1st Century Synagogues in Judea

Perhaps most importantly the archaeological evidence demonstrates that there were, indeed, distinct synagogue buildings and that they could be close to the Temple. Secondly, evidence of Jewish praxis supported their use, especially *mikvah'ot* and the careful collection of 'water from heaven' for ritual immersion.

The construction of synagogues by rebels, patriots and zealots on Massada and Herodium, under almost seige conditions, attest to their importance to the Jewish defenders who took refuge there. This conclusion is supported by the fact that they built one *mikvah*, or more, at each location.

In the villages synagogues were large and were built close to residences, which confirmed their importance, however, their large size and prominence increased their attraction as targets for Roman destruction.

(2) Conclusions About Jewish Praxis in Galilee

The Magdala Synagogue provides useful evidence of ritual activity. There were four *mikva'ot* and a special quarter of the town apparently used for cultic/religious purposes. One room in this section of the town had a mosaic floor featuring a rosette and stone benches along the back, as though it was an important meeting room.

Other finds included: stone vessels such as priests used, a shovel for ash, the ornamented *Aron HaKadosh*, the fully carved 'Magdala stone' in the main hall and the plain chalk stone in the 'study room'. Both stones probably facilitated either prayer as the excavators supposed85 or Scripture reading in public or in private as Mordechai Aviam proposes.86 If one combines this with evidence from Cana (the biblical story of the huge stone jars for purification at the wedding of Cana as well as the synagogue there, with its adjacent *mikvah*) a sense of particular observance and devotion in the Galilee emerges. The symbols carved on the Magdala stone reveal a close connection with the Temple. Different scholars interpret them differently but all seem to relate the symbols back to the Temple.

(3) Conclusions About Jewish Synagogue Buildings in Galilee

Synagogues built in the North before the Roman destruction of 70 CE are very significant. The basalt example in Capernaum (beneath the famous limestone example) is the largest, but Gamla and Khirbet Cana are almost as large. Even small villages built large synagogues and both those at Capernaum and Gamla may have been two storeys high. Pools for ritual immersion were built close by (as at Kiryat Sefer, Modi'in, Gamla, Khirbet Cana and Magdala).

The Magdala synagogue is in remarkably good condition and the iconography carved into the Magdala stone challenges the opinions of many of the critics and Bible-sceptics about both Galilee being populated by gentiles and about synagogues being merely meeting-places, not buildings.

Early synagogues were large, simple and rustic.

After a post-destruction period of a century or more synagogues began to be built once more. These synagogues, such as Kfar Bar'am, were more elaborate and had more decorations and more refined architecture.

As was previously suggested in the cases of Modi'in in Judea and Gamla in the Golan Heights, synagogues were built, rebuilt and renovated. In fact the first archaeologists of the Israel Antiquities Authority working at Magdala (Dina Avshalom-Gorni and then Arfan Najar) reported that the Magdala synagogue had been built over foundations from the Hasmonaean period. There is also an opinion that Magdala was renovated and enlarged in c.40 to 43 CE (just after 'the Jesus period').87 This suggests an increase in use by the Judeo-Christians of that part of the Galilee.

Organised instruction about Judaism, which was a complex cult, would have encouraged allegiance to the Temple and Jerusalem but synagogue activities would also have enhanced village harmony, solidarity and unity, even if the content spoken there had not always been Torah-centred. It has to be noted, however, that Jews were not dualists, that is, they did not separate the sacred from the secular (as Christians tend to do). All of life formed part of their Judaism, which was a total way of life and they made no distinction between secular and sacred activities.

(4) General Conclusions

As the Theodotus inscription indicates, synagogues were very important in Jerusalem, as they also were in small villages and on rural estates. They were carefully positioned: in the town square (Kiryat Sefer), near the city gate (Gamla), in the centre of town (Modi'in) and on the summit of the hill (Khirbet Cana and the public building/ synagogue at Horvat 'Ethri). Some date back before the turn of the eras (Modi'in, Kiryat Sefer and Gamla) and some, such as Massada, Herodium, Magdala and the basalt building at Capernaum, can be dated to the 1st century CE. Tel Rechesh, Shuafat and Horvat 'Ethri may not be securely dated but they are most likely to be 'pre-destruction' in date, in a period of relative peace when farming would have been prosperous. Coin-finds and potshards are the main methods of dating but new technologies are becoming useful, as used, for example, by the American excavators during the excavation of Khirbet Cana.

Evidence of efforts to decorate synagogues internally has survived: mosaic floors and colourful wall-painting being the main decorations in the 1st century.

Judging by the customary seating arrangement, discussions, or listening to speakers, preachers or readers of the *Torah*, were the prime reasons for their initial construction: *"Research indicates that Torah reading and study were the chief religious activities in the synagogue during the Second Temple period".*[88]

Synagogues did not compete with the Temple in size or beauty, being simple, rustic and built of local stone, whereas the Temple was beautiful, with gleaming white limestone and imported marble embellished with gold and silver. As Jewish Law (*Halakah*) required, synagogues differed markedly from the Temple in appearance and ritual. Within Israel there was no hint of any outside sacrifices because Ex. 29:42-46 forbad sacrifices except at the Tabernacle/Temple.

Within Israel, synagogues actually facilitated the work of the Temple in many ways: by collecting and transferring the Temple-tax to Jerusalem, by encouraging pilgrimage for the three pilgrim festivals and by enhancing the inclusion of local people as participants in the rituals and other cultic activities. A deputation of local people went with the local priest when it was his turn to serve in the Temple, and appropriate scripture portions were read in the home-synagogue at that time, by way of moral support.

Primarily, synagogues were established to teach each generation the beliefs and rituals of Judaism, which nourished Temple praxis.

These synagogues, especially those excavated since 1990, are very important because they challenge old assumptions and assertions (based upon the lack of evidence that was interpreted to mean that no evidence would be found). Such older conclusions included: that synagogues were not dedicated buildings but only meeting-places;[89] that they were only built in remote places (like Egypt and Galilee) where Jews had no access to the Temple; that any synagogue in Jerusalem (such as the Theodotus synagogue and the Biblical *"synagogue of the freed-men"*) would have been ignored by native Jews in favour of the Temple but were for strangers and foreigners who came from distant lands and that such synagogues were therefore not important institutions.[90] A previously adopted conclusion, that there was competition and/or disharmony between synagogues and the Temple, cannot be substantiated and the longevity of the Theodotus synagogue over three generations and its proximity to the Tempe suggests otherwise.

Each significant excavation demonstrates that many well-known scholars were forced into error through lack of hard evidence although the same may well be said of this generation of scholars in decades to come, depending upon what may be found in the future. Scholars can only interpret what they have at hand.

The existence of 1st-century synagogues in Judea, Galilee and the Golan Heights has been established, which supports the Gospels' numerous claims that they were *"throughout Galilee"* and when new synagogues are discovered they provide an ever-growing body of evidence to excite academic study.

The synagogue as an institution flourished because it fulfilled community needs which the Temple was not designed to fulfil. A discussion of various 'sacred' and 'secular' activities which took place there is available in our book *Synagoga's Heritage: Tabernacle, Temple, Synagogue and Church.*[91] Although modern scholars are not necessarily aiming to do so, their findings increasingly demonstrate support for what the New Testament recorded about the prevalence and importance of synagogues in Jewish communities in Judea and the Galilee.

Appendix I.
Post-destruction Synagogues

i. David's Tomb

Tourists and Pilgrims flock to see the Cenacle or Coenaculum (dining room) in Jerusalem but it is a Crusader era building, from the 12th Century. Beneath it, however, are the original floor and some walls of a much earlier building. It began life as a synagogue in the decades between the two Jewish Wars and was not destroyed by the Emperor Hadrian when he razed Jerusalem because it was outside the city-confines.

Appendix Plate 1.
1st century Judeo-Christian synagogue, 1864.

Now known as David's Tomb. Public domain.[92]

This humble rectangular room was built on 1st-century remains, dated 'after 70 AD but before the Bar Kokhba revolt'.

and its original northeastern, western walls and its northwestern corner have survived to a few meters[93] also: *"some of the pillars which formed the base of the arches that marked at least six bays of the church (have survived)"*[94]

'David's Tomb' has changed little over the centuries, although two more levels of flooring have been laid over the original stone pavement. a partition has been created across the middle and one wall has been rebuilt in the wrong place, so that the niche is no longer in the centre of the end wall.[95] This central niche for Torah scrolls is not a floor-length apse (see Appendix Plate 2).

This building is still important to the three faiths and it has been saved from destruction because an Islamic minaret was erected on it, and it has long been identification as David's tomb.[96] The erection of a minaret on the building by the Turks and its identification as David's tomb.

Originally, Judaeo-Christianity was mainstream and shared communion with all believers, up until the time of Bishop Soter of Rome (c.157-174)[97] but the memory of all things Judaeo-Christian was largely dropped from history as Latin Christianity grew. The Latin Church was predominantly gentile and expanded to dominate the Christian landscape so that Jewish observances were denounced by bishops (such as John Chrysostom) and forbidden by various Councils, beginning with Nicaea in 325 C.E..[98]

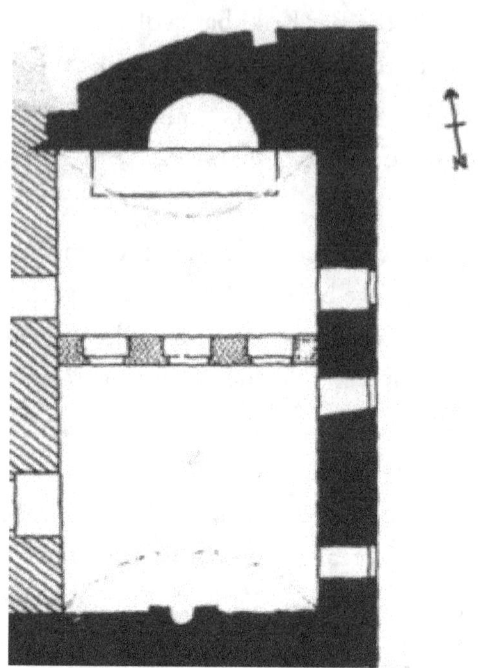

Appendix Plate 2.

Plan of 'David's Tomb'. [99]

An Inscription was found which suggests that it was a Judaeo-Christian Synagogue. When Jacob Pinkerfeld, an archaeologist, was studying the sub-floor levels in 1951 he discovered two Greek graffiti scratched onto plaster. They were first published by Bagatti in his *Church of the Circumcision* (1971) and translate: "" *Conquer, Savior, mercy*" and "*O Jesus, that I may live. O Lord of the autocrat*" . If correctly dated, these would be the oldest Christian inscriptions known in Israel and certainly the oldest to name Jesus. This ancient graffiti indicates that the building belonged to the early Jewish believers in Jesus Christ as Saviour.

Now the famous upper room, the Cenacle, with its 12th century Crusader arches is displayed as the room of the Last Supper and of the birthplace of *Ecclesia* (the Church) at Pentecost but its floor, walls and ceiling are not from the 1st century. By contrast, the humble rectangular room below it preserves late-1st-century and Byzantine Era remains, including parts of its north, north-eastern and western walls (see Appendix Plate 2).

Unlike Constantine's great 4th century basilics 'David's tomb' is small, simple, undecorated, functional, intimate and inexpensive for a close-knit group of believers who met in small, simple, intimate places.

ii) Bar' Am Synagogue

It is most improbable that new synagogues were built for at least a century after the Roman destruction of 70 C.E. although some were repaired and continued in use until the second destruction that occurred during the Bar Kokhba uprising of 132-135 C.E. As noted above, many thousands of men of fighting age were killed and many people in general were taken away as slaves so that big projects would have been impossible. Repairs to houses would have been the priority. Families were shattered, orderly social life and economic activities were destroyed and morale suffered because of the thorough destruction of the Temple in Jerusalem, *"no stone being left upon another"* (Lk. 21:6). It is a tribute to the spirit of the remaining Jewish leaders that Rabbinic Judaism arouse out of the chaos to chart a way forward.

When new synagogues eventually began to be built they were quite different, perhaps influenced by contemporary Christian buildings (examples of which include 'David's Tomb', the *domus ecclasia* at Dura-Europos and the Chapel of the Centurion, Gaianus, at Legio near Meggido).[100] The 'Galilee style' was not rebuilt, replaced by rectangular buildings with a flat floor and in which people sat on wooden benches or chairs facing the front, or upon *triclinia*, in the Roman style.

Appendix Plate 3. Kfar Bar'am in Northern Galilee. Public domain.

In the far North, near the border with Lebanon, a fine example of the new style has survived sufficiently for the decorative entablature and carved inscriptions to be admired and the floor-plan to be obvious.

Covered porticos were introduced. Triple entrances were built, with the central doorway being taller, wider or more splendid, as was invariably the case in the Byzantine churches that have survived.[101]

The synagogue of Bar'am, is dated second-to-third century and is one of the first in the new style. It is currently being restored but is endangered by rocket fire from Lebanon. The new style resembled basilica-style churches in which the congregation faces the front. Internal rows of columns held up the roof and the floor was all level. The three front doors at Bar'am also resemble the usage of churches and there was a columned open narthex (a rectangular porch) across the full width of the front; as basilica-churches had. Four columns of the narthex are still standing.

Because of the extreme persecution of Early Christians in the Levant, only archaeological remains have survived to tell the tale of those churches, although the historian Eusebius, who personally witnessed persecutions and wrote detailed descriptions, assures us that there were churches before Constantine and Helena began to build theirs, which included the Holy Nativity in Bethlehem and the Holy Sepulchre in Jerusalem.

Appendix 2. Where Did Synagogues Originate?

In the first century, the Jewish philopopher of Alexandria, Philo, in *Embassy to Gaius* 155-157; 311-313, recorded that synagogues in Asia and Italy collected and sent money to the Temple. So there were certainly synagogues in the Diaspora while the Temple stood (i.e., before it was destroyed in 70 C.E.) but which are the oldest?

At City Gates in Israel

According to II Sam. 19:8 and I Kings 22:10, some kings sat at city gates to dispense judgements. Other gatherings of citizens took place there (Ruth 4: 1-6) so that some scholars propose that synagogues formed there: virtually out of doors. Although there is archaeological evidence for city gates, even six-chambered gates, evidence for Torah teaching and/or prayer is lacking.

In Babylon

Traditionally scholars have believed that the synagogue as an institution was developed during the Babylonian captivity of Judea, after the destruction of the First Temple in 587 B.C.E. Because there is no extant evidence this view has lost support.[102] Certainly the prophet Jeremiah wrote from Jerusalem to the exiles in Babylon giving them instructions on how to live in exile. They were to plant, eat, build, marry, have children and grandchildren, pray and seek peace and prosperity for the city of their refuge (Jer. 29:4ff): in other words, to remain Jewish but to settle there. It is logical to assume that Jews had communal meetings of a cultic or religious nature as they preserved their racial identity in Babylon. During this period of Jewish exile serious scholarship included the editing of the Book(s) of Kings, based upon archival material, and the prophets Ezekiel and perhaps Daniel stirred the people to desire a return to Zion, as expressed, for example, in Psalm 137.

In Egypt

In 1949-1960 the famous archaeologist W. F. Albright noted 'synagogues' in Egypt dated to the 3rd-century B.C.E.,[103] but since 1987 scholars have paid more attention to possible Egyptian origins of the synagogue because of the work of J. Gwyn Griffiths.[104] Two inscriptions each memorialise the founding of a proseuche (place of prayer) which may not have been a synagogue. The purpose of the latter was educational: teaching Torah, as the Theodotus inscription states.

Other scholars, however, look further afield, for example to Rome, Delos or Ostia, for the oldest such buildings.

On the island of Delos

The Delos remains scattered around this Greek island are dated 250 B.C.E. by Steve Rudd but to the 2nd century B.C.E. by Brian Schaefer. Either way they might predate any synagogue-remains in Israel. One extant Greek inscription of the Delos building reads:

"The Israelites on Delos who make first-fruit offerings to the temple on holy Mt.Gerizim honour Menippos, son of Artemidorus, of Herakleion, both himself and his descendants, for constructing and dedicating his own funds for the proseuche of God, the ... and crown him with a gold crown...."[105]

The mention of Mt. Gerizim probably indicates that it was a Samaritan synagogue, but it is logical to think that Jews built synagogues equally early, or earlier.[106] Jews were on Delos at the time, but did they also build a synagogue on Delos?

In Rome

Jewish burials in Roman catacombs provide rich evidence for a Jewish population in Rome of perhaps 40,000 people (10% of the city) and of twelve different synagogues and of 543 named buried individuals. Known burials date from the 2nd century B.C.E to the 4th century C.E.[107] Although the largest Jewish catacomb, Monteverdi, has been destroyed by the building of apartments, many inscriptions have survived in museums in the Vatican, Berlin, Rome, Oxford and New York.[108]

In Ancient Rome, the chief synagogue official was called an '*archisynagogus*'. The '*hyperetes*' looked after the buildings and the '*archigerosiarch*' led the community.[109] Rabbis are not mentioned, but without rabbis, exposition of Scriptures may not have taken place.

Obviously, synagogues acted as burial societies.

The ceilings and walls of Jewish catacombs in Rome are decorated with Jewish iconography and a few similarly decorated sarcophagi have survived. The menorah is the symbol must often used. The inscriptions are in Latin or poorly spelled Greek, which suggests only elementary education and therefore a lower income. Many would have been freed slaves from Pompey's harrying of the Levant in 63 B.C. This may have been the same demographic as members of the 'Synagogue of the Freedmen' of Acts 6:9.

In Ostia

Ostia was a port city at the mouth of the Tiber River and thus closely connected with Rome so that what applied in one city probably applied in the other, with Rome taking the lead. It is not, therefore, surprising to find a Jewish community in Ostia: but certainly not twelve congregations (as found in Rome).

The Ostia synagogue is relatively intact and is dated to the reign of emperor Claudius (41-54 C.E.) although it underwent many changes until the 5th century.

Its earliest form included a main hall with benches along three sides, a monumental gateway with four marble columns, a dining room (a triclinium with couches along three walls for reclining) a well and an external basin for handwashing (as also found at Magdala).

Communal meals were also a feature of synagogue-life in Rome. The Jewish historian Josephus recorded that a decree of Emperor Augustus of 2-3 C.E. made the sacred moneys of the Jews inviolate and incidentally indicates that Jews had banqueting halls, as indicated by this text: Money *"may be sent to Jerusalem and delivered to the treasurers in Jerusalem, and that they need not give bond* (to appear in court) *on the Sabbath or on the day of preparation for it after the ninth hour* (c.4:00 p.m.). *If anyone is caught stealing their holy books or holy monies from a synagogue* (a sabateion) *or a banqueting hall* (an andrōn)[110] *he shall be regarded as sacrilegious* (i.e., a temple-robber) *and his property shall be confiscated,"* (*Antiquities* 16:162-73).

Athough Ostia is cited as the oldest extant synagogue in Europe those of Rome were one or two centuries older, although now lost, leaving only their names in the catacombs.

In Jerusalem Under Ezra

When the deportees returned from Babylon to Judea it became obvious to the scribe-priest Ezra that many of them were ignorant of Torah. Some could not understand Hebrew and some had intermarried with foreigners and so were partly assimilated to Babylonian lifestyles and culture. Ezra soon took steps to rectify this lack, by public readings of Torah, but an ongoing teaching process would also have been required. Although there is no Scriptural warrant for a prolonged, organised, ongoing effort to encourage Sabbath keeping, Torah knowledge and observance of the Levitical Feasts, this was needed. Every step in that direction, in small or large gatherings, in-doors or in public, was a move towards the synagogue of 'the Jesus Period'.

BIBLIOGRAPHY

Primary Sources

Jerusalem Talmud,

The Mishnah

1 Maccabees

Josephus, *Vita*

Josephus, *Wars of the Jews*

Josephus, *Antiquities of the Jews* .

Eusebius, *The History of the Church: from Christ to Constantine*

Media Sources

Ha Aretz, 17/8/2014, 'Hoard of Bronze Coins From the Jewish Revolt Found Near Jerusalem', by Ron Shapiro.

The Times of Israel, 'A 2000 year old murder leads to an illicit burial in the heart of the West Bank', by Amanda Borschel-Dan,

www.timesofisrael.com/a-2000year-old-murder-leads-to-an-illicit-burial-in-the-heart-of-the-West-Bank

Ynetnews 14/8/2016, 'Ancient synagogue discovered in Galilee', by Yitzhak Tessler,

ynetnewscom/articles/0,7340,L-4841.308,00.html

Secondary Sources

Adler, Yonatan, 'The myth of the osar in Second Temple-period ritual baths: anachronistic interpretation of a modern-era innovation', *Journal of Jewish Studies* 65 (2014), 263-283.

Albright, W. F., The Archaeology of Palestine (Harmondsworth: Penguin, 1949/1960).

Bauckham, Richard, 'Further Thoughts on the Migdal Synagogue Stone', *NT* 57.2 (2015).

Bauckham, Richard (ed.), The Book of Acts in its Palestinian Setting (Grand Rapids, 1995).

Cameron, A. and A. Kuhrt, *Images of Women in Antiquity* (London: Croom Helm, 1983).

Campbell, Justin and Deslee Campbell, Synagoga's Heritage: Tabernacle, Temple, Synagogue and Church *(Xlibris, 2020).*

Chancey, M. and E. Meyers, 'How Jewish Was Sepphoris in Jesus' Time? Spotlight on Sepphoris', *Biblical Archaeology Review* 26.4. *(July-Aug., 2000), 18-34.*

Charlesworth, James H. (ed.), Jesus and Temple: Textual and Archaeological Explorations *(Fortress Press, 2014).*

Coltheart, David, 'The 2000 Dig at Hoah', *Archaeological Diggings* 7.5 (Oct./Nov., 2000), 3-9.

Dacy, Marianne Josephine NDS, 'The Separation of Early Christianity from Judaism,' Ph.D. thesis, University of Sydney (June, 2000).

Fiensy, David and James Strange (eds), Galilee in the Late Temple and Mishnaic Periods, *Vol. 2:* The Archaeological Record from Cities, Towns and Villages (Fortress Press, 2015).

Fine, Steven (ed.), Jews, Christians and Polytheists in the Ancient Synagogue (London and NY: Routledge, 1999).

Flesher, Paul Virgil McCracken, 'Palestinian Synagogues Before 70 C.E. A Review of the Evidence' *Journal of Theological Studies* (1987),

Grabbe, Lester L., 'Synagogues in pre-70: A Reassessment,' *Journal of Theological Studies New Series 39:2 (1988).*

Griffiths, J. Gwyn, 'Egypt and the Rise of the Synagogue', *Journal of Theological Studies* 38.1 (1987).

Hachlili, Rachel, Ancient Jewish Art and Architecture in the Land of Israel (Leiden: Brill, 1988)

———'The Origin of the Synagogue: A Reassessment', *Journal of Theological Studies 28.1 (1997).*

———'Synagogues Before and After the Roman Destruction of the Temple', *BAR* 41.3 (2015).

Katsnelson, Natalya, 'Baba El-Gharbiya Area: The glass vessels from Nahal Hadera (North)', *Atiqot* 64 (2010).

———'The Coins from Kh. Bad 'Isa, Qiryat Sefer: New Archaeological Evidence', Biblical Archaeologist *46, 210ff.*

Kee, Howard Clark, 'The Transformation of the Synagogue after 70 C.E. Its Import for Early Christianity,' *New Testament Studies 36 (1990), 1-24.*

Knox, Alan, 'The church, the synagogue and the city gates' *Gatherings,* Nov. 12, 2012.

La Sor, William S., 'Discovering What Jewish Miqva'ot Can Tell Us About Christian Baptism', *BAR (*Jan/Feb, 1987), 54.

Levine, L. I. (ed.), *Ancient Synagogues Revealed* (Jerusalem/Detroit: I.A.A., 1981).

Levine, Lee I., The Ancient Synagogue: The First Thousand Years *(2nd ed.)* (New Haven: Yale University Press, 2005).

Lim, Timothy H., The Dead Sea Scrolls: *A Very Short Introduction* (Oxford: Oxford University Press, 2005).

Marshall, I. H. et al. (eds), *The New Bible Dictionary* (3rd ed.) (Leicester, England: IVP, 1996/2007).

Muncaster, Ralph O., Can Archaeology Prove the Old Testament? (Eugene, Oregon: Harvest House, 2000).

Netzer, Ehud, Massada III. The Yigael *the* Yadin Excavations 1963-1965, Final Reports (Jerusalem, 1991) 402-413.

———'A Synagogue from the Hasmonean Period Recently Exposed in the Western Plain of Jerico', *Israel Exploration Journal 49 (1999), 2-28.*

Onn, Alexander et al., 'Khirbet Umm el-'Umdan', *Hadashot Arkeologiyaot, IAA. 14 (2002).*

Onn, Alexander and Weksler-Bdolah, 'Khirbet Umm el-'Umdan', *Hadashot Arkeologiyaot,* IAA. 14 (2002).

Onn, A. and S. Weksler-Bdolah, 'Modi'in: Hometown of the Maccabees', *BAR* Mar./Apr. 2014, 18-22.

Onn, Alexander and Y. Rafyunu, 'Jerusalem: Khirbet a-Ras', *Hadashot Arkeologiyot* 100:61 (1993), in Hebrew;

Olssen, Berger & Magnus Zetterholm, The Ancient Synagogue From Its Origins until 200 C.E. (Stockholm, 2003).

Reich, Ronny, 'The Hot Bath-House (*balneum*), the Miqweh and the Jewish Community in the Second Temple Period', *Journal of Jewish Studies* 39.1 (1988),

Ristine, Jennifer, *Mary Magdalene: Insights from Ancient Magdala* (Jerusalem: Magdala Institute, 2018).

Runesson, Anders, Donald D. Binder and Birger Olsson, *The Ancient Synagogue from its Origins to 200 C.E., A Source Book*, (Leiden - Boston, Brill, 2008).

Shanks,Hershel,*Judaism in Stone* (Harper and Row, London and N.Y., 1979).

Strange, James F. and Hershel Shanks, 'Synagogue Where Jesus Preached Found at Capernaum', *BAR 9.6* (1983), 24-31 (also 2008).

Yadin, Y. Massada: Herod's Fortress and Zealot's Last Stand *(London: Wedenfeld, 1966).*

Zissu, Boaz and others, 'Identification of Ancient Modi'in and Byzantine Moditha – Towards a Solution of a Geographical-Historical Issue', 'Atedrah b-toldot Erets-Yisrael e-yishuvah, Jan., 2007.

Zissu, Boaz and Amir Ganor, 'Horvat 'Ethri - A Jewish Village from the Second Temple Period and the Bar Kokhba Revolt in the Judean Hills', *Journal of Jewish Studies 60.1 (2009).*

Electronic Sources

Avshalom-Gorni, Dina and Arfan Najar, 'Migdal' in *Hadashot Archeologiyot* 125 (2013)

http://www.hadashot-esi.org.il/report_detail-eng.aspx?id=2304 [1]

Catacomb Society, 'Jewish Catacombs of Rome'

http://www.catacombsociety.org/jewish-catacombs-of-[2]rome/ [3]

---

1.   http://www.hadashot-esi.org.il/report_detail-eng.aspx?id=2304

2.   http://www.catacombsociety.org/jewish-catacombs-of-rome/

3.   http://www.catacombsociety.org/jewish-catacombs-of-rome/

Hebrew University of Jerusalem, 10/8/2016, 'Rare frescoes from the Roman period discovered at Zippori in the Galilee,'
sciencedaily.com/reeasses/2016/08/16081011390/htm

Encyclopedia.com, 'Sepphoris'.
https://www.encyclopedia.com/religion/encyclopedias-almanacs-[4]transcripts-and-maps/sepphoris [5]
Hasson, Nir, 'Archaeologists in Israel Find Ancient Synagogue Predating Second Temple Ruin', in Haaretz 15/8/2016.
https://www.aaretz.com/jewish/archaeology/1.736752
'Kiryat Sefer': A Synagogue in a Jewish Village of the Second Temple Period',
http://www.mfa.gov.il/mfa/israelexperience/history/pages/kiryat%[6]20sefer%20-[7]%20a%20synagogue%20in%20a%20j[8]ewish%20village%20of.aspx
Hachlili, Rachel, 'Synagogues Before and After the Roman Destruction of the Temple', *BAR* 41.3 (2015).
cojs.org/synagogues-before-and-after-the-roman-destruction-of-the-Temple
Onn, A. and S. Weksler-Bdolah, 'Khirbet Umm el-'Umdan,' HA-ESI 118 (2006).

---

4.   https://www.encyclopedia.com/religion/encyclopedias-almanacs-trnscripts-and-map0s/sepphoris

5.   https://www.encyclopedia.com/religion/encyclopedias-almanacs-trnscripts-and-map0s/sepphoris

6.   http://www.mfa.gov.il/mfa/israelexperience/history/pages/kiryat%20sefer%20-%20a%20synagogue%20in%20a

7.   http://www.mfa.gov.il/mfa/israelexperience/history/pages/kiryat%20sefer%20-%20a%20synagogue%20in%20a

8.   http://www.mfa.gov.il/mfa/israelexperience/history/pages/kiryat%20sefer%20-%20a%20synagogue%20in%20a

http://www.hadasot-⁹esi.org.il/
Report_Detail_Eng.asx?id=321&mag_id=111 [10]

Schaefer, Brian, 'Investigating the So-called Ancient Synagogue of Delos, Greece.'

https://www.haaretz/archaeology/.premium-[11]what-is-the-ancient-synagogue-of-delos-1.5400594 [12]

Taylor, Joan E., 'The Women Therapeutae and the divided space of the synagogue,'

J.E.Taylor-torreys.org/Sbi/papers2015/
Taylor_women_Therapeutae.pdf

Weksler-Bdolah, Shlomit, 'Khirbet Umm el-'Umdan', *Hadashot Arkheologiyot Excavations and Surveys in Israel*, 'Final report', 126 (2014).

http://hadashot-esi.org.il/Report_Detail_Eng.aspx?id=14718 111

---

9.   http://www.hadasot-esi.org.il/Report_Detail_Eng.asx?id=321&mag_id=111

10.   http://www.hadasot-esi.org.il/Report_Detail_Eng.asx?id=321&mag_id=111

11.   https://www.haaretz/archaeology/.premium-what-is-the-ancient-synagogue-of-delos-1.5400594

12.   https://www.haaretz/archaeology/.premium-what-is-the-ancient-synagogue-of-delos-1.5400594

End Notes

1 Paul Virgil McCracken Flesher, 'Palestinian Synagogues Before 70 C.E. A Review of the Evidence' (hereafter 'Review') *JTS* (1987), p. 39.

2 For example, Howard Clark Kee, 'The Transformation of the Synagogue after 70 C.E. Its Import for Early Christianity,' *NTS* 36 (1990), p.5.

3 Ehud Netzer, ''A Synagogue from the Hasmonean Period Recently Exposed in the Western Plain of Jerico' *IEJ* 49 (1999), 2-28.

4 Since a deep moat has been unearthed between Orphel and David's City in 20-24, the two have begun to be separated, in scholarship.

5 Lester L. Grabbe, 'Synagogues in pre-70: A Reassessment,' *JTS* New Series 39:2 (1988), p. 410.

6 *Loc. cit.* Grabbe, accepts a pre-70 construction date, p. 410.

7 *Jerusalem Talmud, Megillah* 3:1 and 73d and *Ketubot* 13:1 (either 480 or 460 of them).

8 E. P. Sanders 'Common Judaism and the Synagogue in the First Century', in Steven Fine (ed.), *Jews, Christians and Polytheists in the Ancient Synagogue* (London and NY: Routledge, 1999), p. 16 and f/n. 71 and S. S. Miller, 'The Rabbis and the Non-existent Monolithic Synagogue', *idem.* , p. 58.

9 For persuasive arguments in favour of a pre-destruction date see Rainer Risener, 'Synagogues in Jerusalem', in Richard Bauckham (ed.), *The Book of Acts in its Palestinian Setting* (Grand Rapids, 1995), pp. 194 and 200.

10 Anders Runesson, Donald D. Binder and Birger Olsson, *The Ancient Synagogue from its Origins to 200 C.E., A Source Book*, (Leiden- Boston, Brill, 2008) (hereafter *Source Book*), p. 53. An alternative translation is found in Pieter W. van der Horst, 'Was the Synagogue a Place of Sabbath Worship before 70 CE?,' in Fine (ed.), *op.cit.*, p. 19.

11 1 Maccabees 2:1-9 and 3:1-4.

12 *The New Bible Dictionary*, 3rd edition (I. H. Marshall et al., eds) (hereafter *NBD*) (Leicester, England: IVP, 1996/2007) , *s.v.* Maccabees v. The Hasmoneans.

13 Dimensions are from the excavator's final report. Shlomit Weksler-Bdolah, 'Khirbet Umm el-'Umdan', *Hadashot Arkheologiyot Excavations and Surveys in Israel* (hereafter 'Final report'), 126 (2014), p. 2.

http://hadashot-esi.org.il/Report_Detail_Eng.aspx?id=14718 [Accessed 1/9/2018].

14 Alexander Onn et al., 'Khirbet Umm el-'Umdan', *Hadashot Arkeologiyaot*, IAA. 14 (2002), p. 66 (hereafter Umm el-'Umdan').

15 Weksler-Bdolah, 'Final report', *op.cit.*, p. 3.

16 *Ibid.*

17 Onn et al., 'Umm el-'Umdan', *op.cit.*, p. 66.

18 For details see Runesson, Binder and Olsson, *Source Book, op.cit.*, pp. 57-8.

19 Weksler-Bdolah, 'Final report', *op.cit.*, p. 4. In imperial measurements: 34'5"-37'9"x 28' 3".

20 A. Onn and S. Weksler-Bdolah, 'Modi'in: Hometown of the Maccabees,' (hereafter 'Hometown'), *BAR* Mar./Apr. 2014, pp. 18-22.

21 Weksler-Bdolah, 'Final report', *op.cit.*, p. 4.

22 Onn and Weksler-Bdolah, 'Hometown', *op.cit.*, pp. 18-22.

23 *Rachel Hachlili,* Ancient Jewish Art and Architecture in the Land of Israel *(Leiden: Brill, 1988), pp. 84-86.*

24 Ronny Reich, 'The Hot Bath-House (*balneum*), the Miqweh and the Jewish Community in the Second Temple Period', (hereafter 'Bath-House') *JJS* 39.1 (1988), p. 102.

25 mAvoda Zara *3:4.*

26 *mMegillah* 3:2 and *Berikoth* 24:4.

27 Reich ('Bath-House') *op.cit.,* pages 3 and 4 of the document.

28 A. Onn and S. Weksler-Bdolah, 'Khirbet Umm el-'Umdan,' HA-ESI 118 (2006).

http://www.hadasot-esi.org.il/Report_Detail_Eng.asx?id=321&mag_id=111 [Accessed 1/9/2018].

29 Zissu and others, 'Identification of Ancient Modi'in and Byzantine Moditha – Towards a Solution of a Geographical-Historical Issue', 'Atedrah b-toldot Erets-Yisrael e-yishuvah, Jan., 2007.

30 Josephus, *Ant.* XIII.7.6 (211).

31 Irrespective of which of the 6 most likely sites was the original Emmaus.

32 Eusebius, *H.E.*, III. 11 and 32 and IV.21.

33 No distinction is made here between Clopas and Cleopas, as is the Orthodox and Catholic position.

34 The best candidates for Emmaus are Abu Gosh/Kiriath Jearim and Imaus, near Latrun.

35 Ancient authorities, including the early Syriac and Latin gospels, regarded Clopas and Cleopas as the same person, contra Marshall et al. (eds), *NBD, op.cit., s.v.* Cleopas and *s.v.* Clopas.

36 See James F. Strange, 'Archaeology and Ancient Synagogues up to about 200 C.E.', in Berger Olsson and Magnus Zetterholm, *The Ancient Synagogue From Its Origins until 200 C.E.* (hereafter *Ancient Synagogue*) (Stockholm, 2003), pp. 38-9.

37 'Kiryat Sefer': A Synagogue in a Jewish Village of the Second Temple Period', http://www.mfa.gov.il/mfa/israelexperience/history/pages/ kiryat%20sefer%20-20a%20synagogue%20in%20a%20jewish%20village%20of.aspx

[Accessed 30/4/2017].

38 Ralph O. Muncaster, *Can Archaeology Prove the Old Testament?* (Eugene, Oregon: Harvest House, 2000) .

39 Natalya Katsnelson, 'Baba El-Gharbiya Area: The glass vessels from Nahal Hadera (North)', *Atiqot* 64 (2010) and Natalya Katsnelson, 'The Coins from Kh. Bad 'Isa, Qiryat Sefer: New Archaeological Evidence', *BA* 46, pp. 210ff.

Also see James F. Strange, 'Archaeology and Ancient Synagogues', in Olsson and Zetterholm, *Ancient Synagogue, op.cit.*, pp. 38-9.

40 Boaz Zissu and Amir Ganor, 'Horvat 'Ethri - A Jewish Village from the Second Temple Period and the Bar Kokhba Revolt in the Judean Hills', (hereafter 'Horvat 'Ethri'), *JJS* 60.1 (2009), p. 93.

41 Other examples include at Khirbet el Maqatir in the West Bank and Khirbet Marzouk near the main Jerusalem-Jaffa highway. In a cave complex at Khirbet Maqatir the skeletons of seven young women and one male youth were found beneath a one metre layer of ash. 'A 2000 year old murder leads to an illicit burial in the heart of the West Bank', by Amanda Borschel-Dan in *The Times of Israel*, www.timesofisrael.com/a-2000year-old-murder-leads-to-an-illicit-burial-in-the-heart-of-the-West-Bank [Accessed 1/9/2019]. At Marzouk a jug containing 114 bronze coins had been buried. Ron Shapiro, 'Hoard of Bronze Coins From the Jewish Revolt Found Near Jerusalem', in *Ha Aretz*, 17/8/2014.

At both sites Roman arrow-heads were found. The newest coin found was dated 69 CE.

42 Zissu and Ganor, 'Horvat 'Ethri', *op.cit.*, pp. 99-100.

43 David Coltheart, 'The 2000 Dig at Hoah', *AD* 7.5 (Oct./Nov., 2000), pp. 3-9. Zissu and Ganor, 'Horvat 'Ethri', *op.cit.*, p. 108.

44 Zissu and Ganor, 'Horvat 'Ethri', *op.cit.*, pp. 90 and 92.

45 *Ibid.*, p. 94.

46 W. F. Albright, *Archaeology of Palestine* (Harmondsworth Penguin 1949/1960), p. 174.

47 Yadin, *Masssada: Herod's Fortress and the Zealot's Last Stand* (1966), p.166f. Strangely, although the Qumran site, with its many water installations, was already well known these were not interpreted as *mikvah'ot* at the time. William Sanford La Sor, 'Discovering What Jewish Miqva'ot Can Tell Us About Christian Baptism', *BAR* (Jan/Feb, 1987), p. 54.

48 Ehud Netzer opined that the Massada synagogue had been an animal stall, in E. Netzer, *Massada III. The Yigael Yadin Excavations 1963-1965, Final Reports* (Jerusalem, 1991), pp. 402-413.

49 Hershel Shanks, *Judaism in Stone* (hereafter *Judaism in Stone*) (Harper and Row, London and N.Y., 1979), p. 26.

50 Rachel Hachlili, 'Synagogues Before and After the Roman Destruction of the Temple', (hereafter 'Before and After'), *BAR* 41.3 (2015). cojs.org/synagogues-before-and-after-the-roman-destruction-of-the-Temple [Accessed 21/7/2019].

51 Yonatan Adler, 'The myth of the osar in Second Temple-period ritual baths: an anachronistic interpretation of a modern-era innovation', *JJS* 65 (2014), pp. 263-283.

52 m.Mik. 8.1.

53 By 200 CE women were required to pre-wash all of their body hair before immersing but this may have been a post-destruction rule and/or may have been done in the home.

54 Yonatan Adler, *op.cit.*, pp. 263-283.

55 Y. Yadin, *Massada: Herod's Fortress and Zealot's Last Stand* (hereafter *Massada*) (London: Wedenfeld, 1966), p. 164.

56 Contra Shanks, *Judaism in Stone, op.cit.*, p. 29 and Yadin, *Massada, op.cit.*, pp. 184-86.

57 Fleisher, 'Palestinian Synagogues', *op.cit.*, p. 36.

58 G. Forster, 'The Synagogues at Massada and Herodium', in L. I. Levine (ed.), *Ancient Synagogues Revealed* (hereafter *ASR*) (Jerusalem/Detroit: I.A.A., 1981), pp. 24-9. In this series the 'Jesus period' is considered to be c.7 BCE to c.35 CE.

59 *Lee I. Levine,* The Ancient Synagogue: The First Thousand Years *2nd ed.* (hereafter *Ancient Synagogue*) (New Haven: Yale University Press, 2005), pp. 27.

60 Solomon Zeitlin, cited by Howard Clark Kee, 'The Transformation of the Synagogue after 70 C.E. Its Import for Early Christianity,' *NTS* 36 (1990), p. 3.

61 Rachel Hachlili, 'The Origin of the Synagogue: A Reassessment', *JTS* 28.1 (1997), pp. 41-42.

62 Including Paul Fleischer in 'Palestinian Synagogues' and Rachel Hachlili in 'Before and After', *op.cit.*, n.p.p.

63 J. Gwyn Griffiths, 'Egypt and the Rise of the Synagogue', *JTS* 38.1 (1987), p.5. and Archer, 'The Role of Jewish Women', in A. Cameron and A. Kuhrt, *Images of Women in Antiquity* (London: Croom Helm, 1983), p. 278.

64 Alan Knox, *op.cit.*, on line.

65 There are Old Testament references to singing the Psalms of Ascent as pilgrims journeyed, rejoicing at weddings and in the streets (see Ps. 19:5) which would have been exemplary, and of women singing and dancing in the streets with tambourines and lutes (I Sam. 18:6-7).

66 Josephus, *Vita* 276-81, 294-95, see Runesson, Binder and Olsson, *Source Book, op.cit.*, pp. 10; 76-78. See Josephus, *Wars* 2.461 for its capacity of over 600 people.

67 The scrolls are dated from 200 BCE to 70 CE by Timothy H. Lim, *The Dead Sea Scrolls: A Very Short Introduction* (Oxford: OUP, 2005), p. 38.

See footnote 47 with refeence to immersion pools at Qumran.

68 Lawrence H. Schiffman, 'The early history of public reading of the *Torah*' (hereafter 'public reading'), in Fine (ed.), *op.cit.,* pp. 45-6.

69 Schiffman, 'public reading', in Fine (ed), *op.cit.,* p. 45.

70 References given are 4Q266 5 ii 1-3 = 4Q267 5 iii: 3-5 = 4Q273 2 1 in Schiffman, 'public reading', in Fine (ed.), op.cit., p. 45. The first of these readings can be found in Vermes, Geza (ed. and trans.), CDSS, op.cit., pp. 146-7.

71 Runesson, Binder and Olson, *Source Book*, *op.cit.,* p. 32 and James F. Strange and Hershel Shanks, 'Synagogue Where Jesus Preached Found at Capernaum', *BAR* (2008), pp. 62-72.

72 Josephus, *War*, IV.1.2ff.

73 *Justin Campbell and Deslee Campbell,* Synagoga's Heritage: Tabernacle, Temple, Synagogue and Church *(Xlibris, 2020).*

74 Dina Avshalom-Gorni and Arfan Najar, 'Migdal', Preliminary report 6/8/2013, *Hadashot* Archeologiyot 125 (2013) . http://www.hadashot-[13]esi.org.il/ report_detail-eng.aspx?id=2304 [14][Accessed 25/5/2020].

75 R. Bauckham, 'Further Thoughts on the Migdal Synagogue Stone', NT 57.2 (2015), p. 130.

76 Nir Hasson, 'Archaeologists in Israel Find Ancient Synagogue Predating Second Temple Ruin', in Haaretz 15/8/2016. https://www.aaretz.com/jewish/archaeology/ 1.736752 [15]

77 Yitzhak Tessler, 'Ancient synagogue discovered in Galilee', *Ynetnews* 14/8/2016, ynetnewscom/articles/0,7340,L-4841.308,00.html [Accessed 1/9/2018].

78 Runesson, Binder and Olsson, *Source Book, op.cit.,* pp. 75-6; Alexander Onn and Y. Rafyunu, 'Jerusalem: Khirbet a-Ras', *Hadashot Arkeologiyot* 100:61 (1993), in Hebrew; Levine, *Ancient Synagogue, op.cit.,* p. 72 and Hachlili, *Ancient Synagogues, op.cit.,* p. 39. both cited by Joan E. Taylor, 'The Women Therapeutae and the divided space of the synagogue,' p. 17.

J. E. Taylor-torreys.org/Sbi/papers 2015/Taylor_women_Therapeutae.pdf.

79 Taylor, 'Divided Space', *op.cit.,* p. 17

80 Hebrew University of Jerusalem, 10/8/2016, 'Rare frescoes from the Roman period discovered at Zippori in the Galilee,' sciencedaily.com/reeasses/2016/08/ 16081011390/htm [Accessed 15/10/2019].

81 Encyclopedia.com, 'Sepphoris'. [Accessed 17/7/2019].

---

13.   http://www.hadashot-esi.org.il/report_detail-eng.aspx?id=2304

14.   http://www.hadashot-esi.org.il/report_detail-eng.aspx?id=2304

15.   https://www.aaretz.com/jewish/archaeology/1.736752

https://www.encyclopedia.com/religion/encyclopedias-almanacs-transcripts-[16]and-maps/sepphoris [17]

82 See Zeev Wise,' From Galilean Town to Roman City, 100 BCE-200 CE', in David Fiensy and James Strange (eds), *Galilee in the Late Temple and Mishnaic Periods*, Vol. 2: *The Archaeological Record from Cities, Towns and Villages* (Fortress, 2015).

83 Encyclopedia.com, 'Sepphoris', *op.cit.*, online.

84 See M. Chancey and E. Meyers, 'How Jewish Was Sepphoris in Jesus' Time? Spotlight on Sepphoris', *BAR 26.4.* (July-Aug., 2000), pp. 18-34.

85 Avshalom-Gorni and Najar, 'Migdal Preliminary Report, *op.cit.*, online.

86 Mordechai Aviam 'Reverence for Jerusalem and the Temple in Galilean Society', in James H. Charlesworth (ed.), *Jesus and Temple* (Fortress Press, 2014), p. 139, Fig. 5.9.

87 Jennifer Ristine, *Mary Magdalene: Insights from Ancient Magdala* (Jerusalem: Magdala Institute, 2018), p. 36. Avshalom-Gorni and Najar, 'Migdal', Preliminary report *op.cit., online.*

88 Marianne Josephine Dacy NDS, 'The Separation of Early Christianity from Judaism', Ph.D. thesis, University of Sydney (June, 2000), p. 141.

89 So Howard Clark Kee, *op.cit.*

90 Fleischer, 'Review', *op.cit.*, p. 39.

91 Justin Campbell and Deslee Campbell, *op.cit.*, pp. 197-113.

92 Photograph by Ermete Pierotti, artist and author, printed by Day and Son, printer of plates.

93 Bagatti, *op.cit.*, p. 120f. For dating, see Bergil Pixner in *Biblical Archjaeology Review* 16.3, May/June 1990, p. 25.

94 Dan Bahat, 'Recently Discovered Crusader Churches in Jerusalem', in Yoram Tsafrir (ed.) A *ncient Churches Revealed, op.cit.*, p. 125.

95 Finegan, *op.cit.*, pp. 238-39.

96 Finegan, *op.cit.*, p. 238f. This image is in the public domain.

97 Emmanuel Testa, The Faith of the Mother Church: An Essay on the Theology of the Judaeo-Christians *(Jerusalem: Franciscan Printing Press, 1992), p. 163.*

98 For a discussion see Finegan, *op.cit.*, pp. 232-236.

99 The hatched walls are much later additions.

100 These three early Christian buildings are discussed in Justin Campbell and Deslee Campbell, *Synagoga's Heritage: Tabernacle, Temple, Synagogue and Church*, *op.cit.*

101 Two of the three entrances to the Church of the Nativity in Bethlehem are sealed up, as also seen elsewhere.

---

16.   https://www.encyclopedia.com/religion/encyclopedias-almanacs-trnscripts-and-map0s/sepphoris

17.   https://www.encyclopedia.com/religion/encyclopedias-almanacs-trnscripts-and-map0s/sepphoris

102 The 'in Babylon' theory is now outdated according to the Introduction to Anders Runesson, Donald D. Binder and Birger Olsson, *The Ancient Synagogue from its Origins to 200 C.E., A Source Book*, (Leiden - Boston, Brill, 2008) (hereafter *Source Book*) p. 6 and f/n. 13 and citing A. Runesson, *The Origins of the Synagogue: A Socio-Historical Study* (Stockholm: Almqvist and Wiksell International, 2001), pp. 110-123.

103 W. F. Albright, *The Archaeology of Palestine* (Harmondsworth: Penguin, 1949/ 1960), p. 172.

104 J. Gwyn Griffiths, 'Egypt and the Rise of the Synagogue', *JTS* 38.1 (1987), 1-15.

105 Steve Rudd, 'Ancient Synagogue Inscriptions from Delos, Greece 250BC' www.bible.ea/synagogues/Delos-Greece-synagogue-Greek-inscriptions-origin-[18]a [19][Accessed 22/4/2018].

106 Brian Schaefer, 'Investigating the So-called Ancient Synagogue of Delos, Greece.' Accessed 1/4/2018]. https://www.haaretz/archaeology/.premium-what-is-the-ancient-[20]synagogue-of-delos-1.5400594 [21]

107 Catacomb Society, 'Jewish Catacombs of Rome' http://www.catacombsociety.org/jewish-catacombs-of-rome/ [22] A major Carbon Dating project is currently being undertaken to confirm datings.

108 Gil Zohar, 'Rome's Jewish Catacombs', [Accessed 1/4/2018]. www.jpost.com/Magazine/Romes-Jewish-catacombs-open-briefly-to-the-public-453704

109 'Jewish Rome,' http://www.livius.com/artices/concept/diaspora/jewish-rome/ [23] [Accessed 1/1.2019].

110 Runesson, Binder and Olsson, *Source Book, op.cit.*, pp. 151-2. An alternative translation is 'ark', in Fine (ed.), *op.cit.*, p. 3.

---

18.   http://www.bible.ea/synagogues/Delos-Greece-synagogue-Greek-inscriptions-origin-a

19.   http://www.bible.ea/synagogues/Delos-Greece-synagogue-Greek-inscriptions-origin-a

20.   https://www.haaretz/archaeology/.premium-what-is-the-ancient-synagogue-of-delos-1.5400594

21.   https://www.haaretz/archaeology/.premium-what-is-the-ancient-synagogue-of-delos-1.5400594

22.   http://www.catacombsociety.org/jewish-catacombs-of-rome/

23.   http://www.livius.com/artices/concept/diaspora/jewish-rome/

Don't miss out!

Visit the website below and you can sign up to receive emails whenever Deslee Campbell publishes a new book. There's no charge and no obligation.

https://books2read.com/r/B-A-LSULB-EHCCF

Connecting independent readers to independent writers.

Also by Deslee Campbell

Memorable Christians
Phoebe's Sister's: Women Leaders in Early Christianity
Phoebe's Sisters: Women Leaders in Early Christianity
Phoebe's Sisters : Women Leaders in Early Christianity
Bright Shining Lights of an Earlier Era
Shining Lights of the Reformation
Shining Lights of the Reformation
Remarkable Post-Reformation Christians
Remarkable Post-Reformation Christians
Remarkable Post-Reformation Christians
Modern Christian Martyrs
Modern Christian Martyrs
Modern Christian Martyrs
Modern Christian Martyrs ready.doc
Christian Women We Should Remember
Great Christian Men We Have Forgotten
Great Christian Men We Have Forgotten
Great Christian Men We Have Forgotten
Christian Women Leaders of the 20th Century

Shoah Series
Confronting Holocaust Denial

Standalone
The Topkapi Beggar
Voices From The Silence
Why a Roman Emperor Rebuilt Jerusalem and Jerash
Why a Roman Emperor Rebuilt Jerusalem and Jerash
Stones, Walls and Watchmen
Mothers in Israel
Ecclesia a Long Journey to Tomorrow
St Paul's Olive Tree Metaphor
St Paul's Olive Tree Metaphor
Synagogues of the First Century C.E.

Watch for more at www.synagogueandchurch.com.

About the Author

About the Author

Dr Deslee Campbell, a retired educational psychologist and teacher, is a prolific writer of both fiction and works concerned with history, religion and archaeology. She is particularly interested in art, artefacts and architecture as pathways towards understanding the past. Her doctoral thesis from the University of Sydney is entitled "The Iconography of Women: A Study of Byzantium and the Byzantine-influenced Mediterranean, A.D. 395-1204."

Read more at https://www.youtube.com/@synagogueandchurch911.